My March to Liberation

A Jewish boy's story of partizán warfare

I0892083

Other publications by Paul A. Strassmann:

Information Payoff: The Transformation of Work in the Electronic Age – 1985
The Business Value of Computers – 1990
The Politics of Information Management – 1994
Irreverent Dictionary of Information Politics – 1995
The Squandered Computer – 1997
Information Productivity – 1999
Information Productivity Indicators of U.S. Industrial Corporations – 2000
Revenues and Profits of Global Information Technology Suppliers – 2000
Governance of Information Management Principles & Concepts – 2000
Assessment of Productivity, Technology and Knowledge Capital – 2000
The Digital Economy and Information Technology – 2001
The Economics of Knowledge Capital: Analysis of European Firms – 2001
Defining and Measuring Information Productivity – 2004
Demographics of the U.S. Information Economy – 2004
The Economics of Outsourcing in the Information Economy – 2004

My March to Liberation

A Jewish boy's story of partizán warfare

PAUL A. STRASSMANN

GMU PRESS

My March to Liberation

A Jewish boy's story of *partizán* warfare

First GMU Press Edition 2011

Published by GMU Press
Fairfax, Virginia

Design: Spectrum Creative, LLC, Fairfax, Virginia
Editing: Aden Nichols, Little Fire Editorial Services

Printed and manufactured in the United States of America

Version 2.0 – August 2011

ISBN 978-0-9818779-9-0

Originally published in 2006 as *Paul's War*
Strassmann, Paul A.
Paul's War
1. Biography; 920; 2. History of Eastern Europe; 947
Version 1.0 – February 2006
Library of Congress Control Number: 2006900809

To The Murdered, Unavenged:

Filip Strassmann, grandfather
Anna Strassmann, grandmother
Alexander Weiner, grandfather
Adolf Strassmann, father
Franzi Strassmann, mother
Samuel Altman, uncle
Pavla Altman, aunt
Alica Altman, cousin
Irma Flack, aunt
Jozef Flack, cousin
Alexander Schalk, uncle
Erna Schalk, aunt
Karol Schalk, cousin
Alzbeta Schalk, cousin, and child
Eugen Weiner, uncle

CONTENTS

LIST OF PHOTOGRAPHS, DOCUMENTS, AND MAPS

FOREWORD

A Tale of Six Slovakias

By Mills Kelly, Ph.D.
Director, Global Affairs Program
George Mason University

For more than a millennium, time and political boundaries have engaged in an intricate dance in East Central Europe. When I lived in Slovakia in the mid-1990s, my landlord's mother had resided in six different countries without ever having moved from the house in which she was born. Her home in the Slovak town of Modra was within the Habsburg Empire before the First World War, an area that successively became the Republic of Czechoslovakia in 1918, the Nazi-ruled puppet Slovak Republic in 1939, the reconstituted Czechoslovakia in 1945 (under Communist control after 1948), the Czecho-Slovak Federative Republic from 1990 to 1992, and finally, Slovakia as it exists today.

The events related in *My March to Liberation* should be considered within the context of this geopolitical two-step. Paul Strassmann began his life in the interwar Czechoslovak state, a creation of the Paris Peace Conference that remapped Europe and the Middle East. Following the Munich Pact of 1938, Czechoslovakia began to fracture under pressure from Germany, Hungary, and Poland, all of which had designs on its territory. Included in this mix was a Slovak separatist movement led by the fascistic Hlinka Slovak People's Party, which had sought independence from Czechoslovakia almost since the declaration of the new state in November 1918. When the Wehrmacht invaded the Czech frontier (the Sudetenland) in the spring of 1939, the Slovak sector seceded, forming the first autonomous Slovak state—and promptly entered into a military alliance with Nazi Germany.

The staunchly anti-communist Slovak government, led by Catholic priest turned politician Jozef Tiso, marched in lockstep with Adolf Hitler throughout the war; as a result, thousands of Slovak soldiers fought and died on the Eastern Front. When the tide shifted against the Axis powers, the Slovak military leadership mutinied against their civilian masters, launching what came to be known as the Slovak National Uprising (*Slovenské národné povstanie*, or SNP). The poorly coordinated insurrection began in August 1944, but failing to secure key objectives was quickly and brutally suppressed. Survivors fled to the mountains and joined guerilla bands comprising an odd admixture of nationalists and Communists. The outbreak of the SNP was the event that sent Paul Strassmann first to the village of Selec, and eventually into the forests of Slovakia to fight with these *partizáns*.

After the war, Tiso and his cronies were charged with treason and hanged.

Slovakia, Ancient and Modern

The area around the Slovak city of Trenčín has been inhabited for more than 2,000 years. The fortifications situated along the Váh River at what is now Trenčín mark one of the northernmost outposts of the Roman Empire in Central Europe. Between the sixth and ninth centuries C.E., various Slavic tribes—Czechs, Slovaks, Poles, Serbs, Croats, Slovenes, and others—migrated into Central Europe, settling in lands already occupied by immigrant Germanic tribes.

Slovak nationalist historiography accepts as fact the existence of a Great Moravian Empire (see page 79 in *My March to Liberation*) anchored in the region that now forms the border between Slovakia and the Czech Republic—some even consider this to be the first Slovak state. If we could journey back in time to the ninth century to interview the peasants and nobles who lived in this empire, they certainly would not have called themselves "Slovak." Instead, they would have adopted names tied to the places where they lived or the rulers they served. The first Christian church in what is now Slovakia appeared in the third decade of the ninth century C.E., and so they might have referred to themselves as Christians, to distinguish themselves from those holding to the Roman or other pagan religions.

Around the beginning of the tenth century, the lands now called Slovakia fell under the control of Magyar (Hungarian) invaders and remained part of the Hungarian Kingdom until the end of the First World War. In 1918, the northern territories (which contained the largest Slovak populations) were incorporated into the new nation called Czechoslovakia. The marriage to the Czechs was a rocky one; the most popular Slovak politician of the time, Father Andrej Hlinka, was adamantly opposed to the union of the two peoples in a common state. It was Hlinka's Slovak People's Party that led the separatist movement in 1939, linking Slovakia's destiny with the Nazis.

Slovaks have a habit of referring to the lands encompassed by their country as "Slovakia" back into the mists of time—or at least to the ninth century, but neither is correct. Only in 1919 was there a region technically designated Slovakia, a constituent part of the Czechoslovak state. Thus, Slovakia is a very modern place, one that appeared less than 100 years ago.

Deal with the Devil

Throughout the millennium of Hungarian rule, the Slovak population of the kingdom was subjugated—even after the adoption of a modern constitution in the second half of the nineteenth century. Nevertheless, a small coterie of Slovak intellectuals persistently demanded equal status for the Slovak people. Led by Ľudovít Štúr in the mid-nineteenth century, the Slovak intelligentsia fought unsuccessfully for legalization of the Slovak language and political rights for Slovaks.

The nationalist torch was passed to Father Hlinka when he defied an order banning him from consecrating a small church in the town of Černová in 1908. Hungarian police fired on the crowd outside the church, killing and wounding several dozen people, and took Hlinka into custody. During his stint in prison, the Catholic cleric garnered a reputation as an advocate of Slovak nationalism, an eerie harbinger of the events that catapulted Hitler to power two decades later. Following his release, Hlinka unsuccessfully petitioned the Paris Peace Conference for greater autonomy for Slovaks within the new state of Czechoslovakia. Father Hlinka continued to champion the cause of Slovak equality until his death in 1938.

Hlinka's successor, Father Tiso, was bullied into submission by Hitler, and the resulting puppet Slovak Republic owed its existence to "the protection" of Nazi Germany. Slovaks naively hoped to legitimize their independence when the war was over, when in fact the German leadership intended to dismantle their fledgling republic. Still they persevered, and it was this longing for autonomy and cultural identity—and survival—that motivated Strassmann and his fellow *partizáns*.

It's Always About Religion

The majority of Slovaks today consider themselves to be Catholic, either as practicing members of the faith or as a cultural heritage grounded in its traditions. Prior to the Second World War, as much as three-quarters of the population of the region now known as Slovakia cited "Catholic" as its religious affiliation in census counts. However, this same territory contained substantial numbers of Protestants, Jews, Eastern Orthodox, and Greek Catholic believers. While many Slovaks reflexively refer to the Catholic heritage of their society, it is much more accurate to say that for at least the past four centuries, religious diversity has been the norm in the Slovak lands.

Some of this religious diversity is linked to the heterogeneous ethnic groups that also play an important role in the history of this geographical area. Eastern Orthodox and Greek Catholic worshippers are concentrated in the eastern end of the country and are mostly of Ukranian or Rusyn ethnicity. Protestants are mixed in among the Hungarian minority; there is also a strong contingent of Slovak Protestants. The pre-war Jewish population was scattered across the country from west to east, often living in enclaves called *shtetls* in the farthest eastern regions. Most were deported as part of Hitler's "Final Solution" policy. Today, a few thousand Jews remain in Slovakia, most residing in urban Bratislava.

The power and influence of the Catholic church in Slovak society permeates the events described in *My March to Liberation;* the two most prominent Slovak political leaders from 1913 to 1945 were both Catholic priests. Today Slovakia is an ecumenical society, where religious identification is much weaker than it was in the 1930s, due to four decades of Communist suppression of religion and a general decline in religiosity in Europe. While Catholic politicians were the most prominent figures in the interwar period, today the Slovak Christian Democratic party barely registers in elections.

New Wine in Old Bottles

Visitors to Slovakia today will find two thriving urban centers—the capital Bratislava in the west and Košice in the east. More than 15 percent of the country's population lives in these two cities, and both are industrial centers: Bratislava is a global hub of the automotive industry, while Košice's economy is based largely on steel production. As recently as 2008, Slovakia produced more cars per capita than any country in the world—Bratislava has even been called "Little Detroit." Beyond the pale of the cities, many smaller municipalities dot the landscape; indeed, nearly half the population lives in a town or city of under 5,000. Slovak society remains rooted in traditional village customs and traditions.

The world Paul Strassmann grew up in was very much the same. His family lived near the bustling market town of Trenčín; Bratislava and the nearby metropolis of Vienna (approximately forty miles from Bratislava) were a world away. It would have been very uncommon for residents of the area to travel so far in the 1920s or 1930s, and it is no surprise that Strassmann's worldview (and the worldview of those who lived nearby) was informed largely by what he knew of his own neighborhood.

Even today, cities often empty out on Fridays as workers head back to the countryside. One of Bratislava's nicknames is "the Big Village," though it sports towering office buildings crowned with the logos of multinational corporations.

Uneasy Alliance

Modern Slovakia is firmly rooted in "the West"—meaning the European Union, NATO, the global economic system, and other western institutions. But this is a recent phenomenon. Skepticism about the value of western alignment has a long tradition in Slovak history. Many Slovaks felt abandoned when the post-World War I Paris Peace Conference sanctioned the formation of a Czechoslovak state that denied Slovakian autonomy. In spite of four decades of repressive Soviet-sponsored Communist government, the view that Slovakia's fate might lie in the East rather than the West has not entirely disappeared.

Revisionist History

In the wake of the Second World War, all the peoples of Europe did their best to recast their national narratives to characterize themselves as innocent victims of Nazi aggression. After all, who wants to be one of the bad guys, especially when the bad guys were so *very* bad? Slovaks were no different in this regard, opting instead to focus on the valiant struggles of the Slovak Army and Communist partisans against the Germans once the SNP began in August 1944. Across Slovakia today, statues to these freedom fighters far outnumber the memorials to the Slovak Jews who perished during the war.

But in truth, Slovakia was complicit in the Holocaust. Leaders like Tiso encouraged anti-Semitism and complied with Nazi demands for the removal of Slovak Jews to concentration and death camps. Following his execution, myths sprung up about Tiso's attempts to save Slovak Jews from deportation and death at the hands of the Nazis, replete with fictional estimates of how many Jews the Slovak president "saved," ranging from a few hundred to tens of thousands. Recent research places the number of Jews exempted from transportation by presidential decree at fewer than 1,000. More than 55,000 Jews were sent to the camps by Tiso's functionaries and many more died following the revolt, when the Germans took full control of the Slovak Republic and began systematically murdering Jews in their homes, bypassing the logistical difficulties associated with deportation. It is believed that perhaps as few as 10,000 Slovak Jews survived the war.

Some popular histories of Slovakia's role in the Holocaust take the position that the Slovak government merely transported the Jews to the border, and that it was the Germans who were responsible for their ultimate fate. But the evidence reveals that Slovak authorities were not unaware of what was happening to deported Slovak Jews in Poland and elsewhere; they cannot be absolved of their turpitude.

Living History

Perhaps the most profound lesson we can learn from Paul Strassmann's recollections is just how complicated history can be. Accounts of individual lives, like *My March to Liberation*, help us to understand how difficult it is for one person, one family, or even small groups of people, to survive when a tsunami like the Second World War sweeps away the world they had known. But we also learn how the situations in which they find themselves, the choices they make, and the results of their decisions are intricately connected to the larger world around them—a world that is in a constant state of flux.

Paul Strassmann's story is one of many thousands like it, but we have it here in the voice of the boy who lived through these unimaginable events. Strassmann's narrative reinforces the facts we already know, but its vividness brings history to life in a three-dimensional way that makes his telling of these events all the more memorable and authentic.

First and foremost, this autobiography reveals a young man caught up in a war that was surely far beyond his adolescent understanding. The book begins with the immediacy of reacting to the Nazi takeover of his homeland and his dangerous, though unavoidable, choice of joining up with the partisans hiding out in the woods. He takes us with him on clandestine missions to sabotage troop trains, and we experience his meager existence of little food and less shelter. We rejoice with him as he repeatedly manages to cheat death. This is a story of survival against all odds. Reading this extremely personal and unvarnished account illuminates the difficult choices many Slovaks had to make as they were swept away by the riptide of war.

The second section of the book takes a different and more reflective tone as the author examines his early family life, his community, and the nature of anti-Semitism in his world. Here Strassmann recounts the broader context of the events that eventually led to his involvement with the ragtag guerilla bands opposing the Nazis. He also examines the general political and military situation during and up to war's end. Again, history comes to life as we experience Paul and his family dealing with seemingly impossible circumstances on a daily basis. Strassmann broadens his vision once more in Part III. In this panoramic view, we see how the checkered history of Slovakia and the decisions of its leaders created another layer of chaos. In this section of the book, the author grapples with what was and what should have been; the lessons he derives from his experience remain useful today.

My March to Liberation can be read as a memoir, a history, and a political science primer, and I recommend that you contemplate all of these dimensions as you consider the past, the present, and the future.

May 2011

PREFACE

My parents were murdered by the Nazis in 1945. But Adolf and Frances Strassmann left a legacy: There are seventeen second-, third-, and fourth-generation descendants, and the prospects of the first fifth-generation descendant are not too distant.

One of my grandchildren phoned me to listen to my stories for a school term paper. It occurred to me that there may be others who share this curiosity about the experiences of a teenager who lived through the Second World War from the age of nine to sixteen.

So, here are a boy's recollections, divided into three parts. Part I, *Life with the Partizáns*, recounts my war experiences. Part II, *The Way We Were*, is a sketch of my youth and developmental influences. Part III, *Slovakia*, describes the tragedies that shaped my life until I left my homeland for America.

New Canaan, Connecticut, February 2006

Part I

Life with the Partizáns

JOINING *PARTIZÁNS*

When the Soviet Army started westward after the decisive defeat of the Germans in Stalingrad in February 1943, it was becoming clearer with every succeeding month that it was only a matter of time before the Nazi regime would collapse. Preparations for what everybody called "The End" started in Slovakia early in 1944.

1. Slovakia: Carpathian Mountains Divide the Plains in Poland from the Plain in Hungary. Trenčin Is at the Western Mountain Pass Before the Valley Opens

The hitherto dormant anti-Nazi resistance movements began to organize in order to accelerate the transition to eventual liberation.

Circumstances

My father understood that the relative tranquility of our impoverished and restricted circumstances would come to an end as soon as German rule replaced the government of the Slovak collaborators. He realized that when the war front approached, the Nazis would get rid of as many Jews as possible. The Hlinka Guard would make sure that happened to safeguard the new owners of properties expropriated from the Jews; it was said that dead men couldn't ask for justice or restitution of stolen property. So it was highly likely that we would be eliminated, regardless of whether we possessed "official" papers. What had offered us some margin of protection during the initial deportations in 1942 (resulting in the removal and ultimate extermination of most of the Slovak Jews) would not hold up anymore. The chances of becoming a casualty were increasing, regardless of one's ethnicity. The entire civilian population would suffer heavy losses if my hometown of Trenčín became a defended bastion, as it had been for centuries.

I had no idea what, if any, action Father was planning for the transition to liberation. Because of my youth, I could not be trusted to receive such secrets, although I later found out there were not many. Much of the energy in those times was spent trying to remain as inconspicuous as possible. Years later, my sister shared identical sentiments with me. She never understood what the various approaches to salvation were that we were expected to avail ourselves of. I guess that was so because there were not that many options. Ever since our family had discovered that my sister served as a courier for the Resistance, she was emphatically prohibited from engaging in anything that might compromise the safety of the entire family. All the family's plans about what to do as liberation approached were in my father's head. Without his direction, nothing could happen.

Father was a reserve officer of the Czechoslovak army with the rank of major. He was in uniform when the country mobilized at the time of the Munich betrayal. Czechoslovakia's army prepared for the defense of the homeland. I presume that Father had always maintained his military contacts. When the planning for the anti-Nazi uprising started in March of 1944, I suspect that he was forewarned about any military preparations for liberation. That is only a guess to explain the instant evaporation of all of our contingency plans after the Gestapo suddenly snatched him. He was one of the many people—mostly military officers and suspected conspirators—who were seized during the night after the Slovak National Uprising was launched on August 28, 1944.

Contingency Plan

Father must have known through his contacts within the army that a mutiny would be taking place, although he could only guess when that would occur. Nevertheless, late in the third week of August, he decided to proceed with an exercise to test one of our contingency plans. Father seemed to think the uprising would break out at any moment; pervasive rumors about isolated small-scale *partizán* attacks on Slovak Nazis were on every tongue.

The exercise for "how to escape Germans" involved evacuation to one of the designated villages in the surrounding mountains near the village of Selec. Afterwards, our family dispersed to several peasant homes. Then we just hunkered down, disguised in peasant garb, and tried to blend in with the local population. We remained in that condition for three days—just before the uprising started.

This escape exercise turned out to be a complete failure. First, we were noticed as we arrived in daylight in an uncovered truck that bore the markings of my father's former company—not very stealthy! Selec is a typical Slovak mountain village, where the only road winds through a narrow valley formed by a creek. Any truck climbing up the road was subject to the scrutiny of hundreds of suspicious eyes. Second, there were seven of us. We were initially wearing "city" clothing and could not arrive unseen at our safe houses. Besides, except for a former army buddy of my father's, there were no other villagers willing to take us in. We discovered that having everyone stay together as a group and sleep in the same hayloft was not only unpleasant, but was also too noisy. Compounding the problem was the presence—in the same hayloft—of two Russians, who claimed to be escaped prisoners of war. They did not care to have a large Jewish family compromise their refuge.

Meanwhile, several people in Trenčín were wondering where my father had disappeared; his absence was taken as a sign that trouble was imminent. As the uprising had not yet begun, and with our blown cover in Selec, Father decided that we must return home. I suspect he was convinced the Slovak Army would do anything to avoid a conflict with the Germans until the Soviets were ready to renew the offensive that had stalled in the Polish plains. Because of the many obligations my father had in Trenčín, as well as the dependency of my grandparents, we returned from the mountain village, I think on the twenty-fourth or the twenty-fifth of August, in the same truck in which we had ridden out to Selec. This is how we mismanaged our first escape option.

The Disaster

Three nights later, the Gestapo swooped in and arrested my father. I was sleeping at the house of a friend at the time. This was not planned; rather, I had remained there as I might otherwise have been caught out after the curfew. In the morning, my father and grandfather Weiner were gone, and I learned that the Gestapo also inquired about my whereabouts. It was a very close call.

My mother went into hiding along with our closest friends, the Kubičeks. The hideout was in a house located in a small, walled garden practically in the center of the town. It was but a few paces from the place where my parents had enjoyed their wedding reception twenty years earlier. I never saw her again. Her hiding place was betrayed a few weeks later and the Nazis snatched her away. According to the International Red Cross, the only record they had for a Františka/Franzi Strassmann was an entry dated the twentieth of November, 1944, that indicated she had been transferred from the concentration camp in Sered, Slovakia to another camp in Ravensbruck, Germany. She was listed as prisoner #84985, category "political-Jewish." I later learned that my mother died of typhus in the camp sometime in the late spring of 1945.

Choices

My sister managed to secure proper identification papers and left Trenčín to disappear in the Bratislava metropolis. That worked for only a short time; a passerby recognized her and informed the police. She was arrested and immediately transported to the concentration camp in Ravensbruck. At the camp, she was briefly reunited with our mother under indescribable circumstances. I did not see her or learn of her fate until she suddenly appeared in Trenčín early in June 1945, an emaciated slave labor camp survivor.

Then the crackdown came. In the wake of the uprising, I received a message to hurry to the house of a man who had been a trusted employee of my father for many years. It had been prearranged that I could stay in his attic. After I arrived at my prescribed hideout the following day, the Gestapo announced that reprisals would be taken against all supporters of the mutiny. Slovak soldiers who did not report back to barracks for disarming by that evening would be designated as deserters and shot. The local Gestapo command also posted notices all over the town, announcing that if they found any *partizáns*, army deserters, or Jews hidden in any house, everyone in the sheltering family would be summarily executed. When these broadsides appeared, the wife of my protector became very frightened and demanded that I leave. She suggested that I take refuge in the bushes growing on the banks of the nearby river Váh during daytime, when searches were anticipated.

In spite of her fears, I was allowed to remain hidden in the attic for another two nights. Early each morning, she hustled me out of the house. She pressed into my hand a sandwich and two peaches and let me out through a hole in the back fence of their garden. It was sunrise when I snuck out through the surrounding fields dressed only in shorts with a cotton belt, a T-shirt, socks, and sandals. Sticking to back alleys through familiar neighborhoods, I worked my way down to the river and concealed myself in thick bushes near a spot that had been popular with lovers in pleasanter times. Each day, I found myself contemplating my fate—I did not like the situation I was in, but I could see no way out.

On the second day, I realized my only option was to stay put during the day and to sneak back to the house after sundown to face the increasingly hostile wife of an obviously hen-pecked husband. By this point in my life, I had already acquired my lifelong abhorrence of any situation in which I had only one choice—especially if that choice was extremely risky. I concluded that returning to my hideout on the second day was unacceptable. But what to do?

Around ten in the morning, I heard short bursts of machine-gun fire coming from the direction of Inovec mountain about twenty miles southeast of my hiding place. At the same time, the awful smell of a nearby sewer pipe dumping offal into the river assaulted my nose. I could sit still no longer! Whether it was out of desperation or cool and rational calculation I will never know, but I made the decision not to return to my "safe house." With nothing more than an instinctive reaction, I concluded that rather than continuing to cower like a cornered animal, I would go where the war was being fought and become a hero.

Escape

At the time, I was perched on the western bank of the Váh, a short distance from the only bridge across the river. I could see a procession of military vehicles moving back and forth across the span. I was sure sentries would be posted to block my passage. Also, across the river was the town of Trenčín, where I was sure to be recognized. The only choice left was to use my belt to secure my belongings to my head and plunge into the river that was flowing southward.

It was early September and the water was at its lowest levels, exposing many sharp rocks forming rapids that threatened to rip my skin and leave deep gashes. As a Jew, my exclusion from the local swimming pool since 1940 now came in handy, for I had mastered the skill of floating down the river with the current as a sporting adventure. So I grabbed a large tree branch for cover and drifted unseen downriver for about an hour. This carried me safely out of range of any observers and into a region where there were only small villages. It was a refreshing swim, actually, and it took my mind off the nightmare of what was happening to my family.

When I emerged from the river, the scenery was serene and peaceful. Peasants were working their little plots as if nothing was amiss. As long as I offered the familiar greeting, "God be with you," I got friendly, if quizzical, smiles in return. It took another four hours to walk to the village of Selec, the location of my family's first aborted hiding place. Father's contingency-testing exercise turned out to be a blessing—I knew where to go next.

Everything I had learned over the years about how to blend into the landscape came back to me in an instant. The rules were simple: Never walk on a road—seek a walkway on the cow-paths behind the village barns; do not talk to strangers; do not give your name to anyone; never offer explanations, even if asked; when hungry, do not pick someone's fruit, and certainly do not steal; always drink plenty of water from a creek, but only if it comes directly from a mountainside; and if pressed, act stupid and confused.

When I arrived at the farmhouse where we had been hidden only a few days ago, I was told that the surrounding hills were filling up with army deserters, and staying in the village would be too dangerous. I was given peasant pants as well as a cloth jacket and provided directions to the cottage of a gamekeeper on Inovec mountain who would surely lend a hand. At nightfall, I finally made it to the cottage, where I met a warm welcome. The gamekeeper knew my father from the military and held him in high regard. Finally, I got my first good night's sleep in a hayrick (a shelter for storing hay to feed the livestock during the winter months).

In the morning, I enjoyed a breakfast of a thick slab of bacon, bread, and prunes, and was told to disappear into the woods for the day and do my best to dodge the Hlinka Guards, who would be searching for deserters. My blood was up, because I could hear occasional rifle fire not too far away.

Seeking *Partizáns*

At noontime, I came across a band of lightly armed Slovak Army soldiers, who were relaxing near a creek. They were headed to central Slovakia, where a liberated Czechoslovak government had just been formed. I begged them to take me along. They responded with a good-natured laugh, saying I wouldn't be of any use to them. As a consolation prize, they gave me a hand grenade on the condition that I would make myself scarce.

The grenade I had been given could be employed as a concussion grenade, a booby-trap, or when a metal collar was slipped on it, as a fragmentation explosive device. At this point, it is important to explain how one uses a Slovak hand grenade. Wound around the ominous black cylinder was a strip of steel banding. The grenade exploded when the coiled strip was unwound. Depending on how many of the five rings were uncoiled, one could control the time between fusing the grenade and the explosion. When only one ring was left, the grenade would go off in exactly one second. Starting with four windings made it possible to throw the grenade into an open door and still get safely away. This was all explained to me in a few sentences. Luckily, I never had the courage to rely on employing such a confusing device without further practice (which as it happens never came).

Later on, when the supply of these lethal contraptions became plentiful, I was advised to always keep an extra grenade in my satchel in case I was wounded. The grisly humor was that if the satchel was properly set up as an easily triggered "pillow," one would not suffer a headache. This advice was accompanied by an admonition that *partizáns* would never be in a position to take care of their wounded. In guerilla warfare, captured prisoners on either side were kept alive only for torture.

Thus armed and with a growing confidence in my martial capabilities, I started threading my way down a steep path in the direction I believed the shots were coming from. When I saw some deer bounding through the forest nearby, I took it as a warning and hid behind a tree. Not far down the path, a tall man was approaching with a weapon slung on his shoulder. It was a Bren gun, a British squad-level machine gun that was a favorite of the infantry. The man was ambling along in a most careless manner.

I leapt out from behind the tree with my hand grenade outstretched and commanded him to put the gun down. He did as I asked. I recognized him: He was John Kartal, a Jewish man of uncertain means and known in the town as a person of inflated pretensions.

He was now on his way to join the uprising, he said, as he hoped to resume his reserve rank as an officer. Apparently, on the first morning of the revolt, the doors to the local armory were thrown open for anyone to take what he or she wished. Kartal had walked out with the best ordnance he could carry.

He cursed when I told him he was heading in the wrong direction. We shared my bacon and decided that we would now march together to make war, as long as I would relieve him from carrying the heavy satchel bulging with ammunition clips for the machine gun.

Finding *Partizáns*

By the end of the day, we finally made it to the edge of the forest near the village of Mnichova Lehota. Below us was a highway running

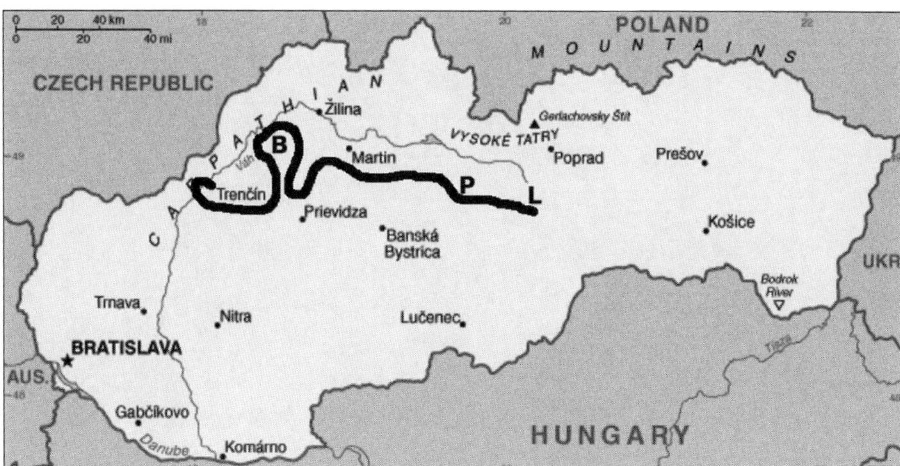

2. Paul's March (black line): B = Base Camps While Attacking Railroad, P = Prašiva, L = Liberation Crossing

alongside the train tracks. John set up the machine gun and asked me to go down the roadway to check out the situation. In a short while, a small pickup truck pulled up and stopped. Suddenly, seven scraggly figures crept out of the woods and headed for the truck. In the lead was a little man with a stump where his left hand used to be; he was sporting a cap with a red star emblem. That's how I met my future leader, Batko. I never knew his first name. He was known as "screw your mother Batko" (sounds better in Russian) because he used that expression to punctuate every few sentences.

I waved for Kartal to come out. He immediately informed Batko that he wished to be transported to the commanding headquarters, where he expected to assume his rightful position as a commissioned officer. The guerilla fighters thought this must be a joke, but Kartal had that Bren gun they coveted, so they held their tongues and loaded us onto the truck. We sped about fifteen miles back to a hamlet called Zavada; it was located on a highway that was heavily patrolled by German vehicles. Such dangerous maneuvers reflected a pattern for what was to come—Batko's approach to guerilla warfare was either utter disregard for operational safety or a boastful demonstration of reckless courage. I was euphoric. I was in the company of armed men who thought only of killing Germans and Hlinka Guards.

And so my *partizán* life began.

THE MINERS

The *partizáns* were returning from cutting the tracks on the feeder rail line leading from Trenčín to the town of Banovce. Everyone was in high spirits.

Comrades

The number two man of the squad was known as "Tato," a Slovak diminutive of the word for "father." He was a grey-haired old Communist and a machinist by trade. He rarely spoke, but when he did, everybody listened. Tato reputedly served in the Spanish Civil War, but nobody could be sure of that. He often argued with Batko over the leader's aggressive tactics, as he did not want to alienate the local population. Tato took Kartal's machine gun and positioned it on top of the cab of the pickup truck to render us combat-ready as we raced down the empty highway—we could have encountered a German motorized patrol at any moment.

I took an immediate liking to such belligerent conduct and also loved the spirit of everyone in the band; they were boisterously pugnacious. Our team included Milos, an athletic engineering student from Moravia. Then there was Ivanko, who claimed to have escaped from a German concentration camp, but was always suspected by our political commissar as a turncoat eager to escape his fate when the war ended. Liška ("little fox") was a local farmer who had problems with his landlord (and the man's wife). Joining *partizáns* seemed to offer a reprieve from all his troubles—little did he know! Although small in stature, he ended up lugging the cumbersome Bren gun after we lost Tato.

Batko spent most of his time with the red-headed Ivanov, a Soviet radio operator and the commissar assigned to keep an eye on us. Ivanov turned out to be a decent and quiet chap who did not go on the raids with us, but took care of all sorts of administrative matters and the mountain of paperwork demanded from headquarters.

Batko was a former professional soldier. He had served with a guerilla outfit somewhere in Byelorussia (now Belarus) that was originally formed by soldiers who took to the hills rather than surrendering to the Germans advancing on Moscow. The bypassed soldiers avoided being taken prisoner by forming loosely knit *partizán* bands. He had been parachuted in to our area of operations a month before by the *partizán* command in Kiev. He was a member of a handpicked group of commandos whose primary mission was to interdict traffic on the main railroad line from Bratislava to Žilina.

As I understood it, when the Soviets liberated territories where there were still some surviving *partizáns*, these tough, highly experienced fighters were immediately redeployed ahead of the advancing Soviets and assigned high-risk missions. After the war, I found out that any Soviet soldier who had survived either as a POW or as a *partizán* was sentenced to hard labor in gulags in Siberia. The simplistic Soviet logic was that if they hadn't died in the defense of Mother Russia, they could never be trusted by the Communist Party.

Induction

When we finally rolled into the village where the *partizán* brigade command post was located, Kartal (having been relieved of the Bren gun) was sent on his way. Meanwhile, Batko had taken a liking to me, even though I did not understand a word he was saying. I suspect it was because I claimed to know all of the mountain trails around Trenčín. This was partially true. I quickly learned that brashness and denial of fear compensated for many shortcomings, including my youth and the fact that I had never actually fired a gun.

After an obligatory swig of gut-searing home-brewed *slivovic* (plum brandy), I was inducted into the little band that was known by the *partizán* headquarters as "Batko's Miners." The designation of "miners" was shorthand for "mine-laying suicidal maniacs." My job was to perform *rozvedka* (reconnaissance), which in plain English meant walking a hundred yards ahead of the squad to trigger unwelcome situations.

Aside from Tato and the Bren gun, only Batko had a fully automatic weapon—a Russian PPSh submachine gun with a drum magazine that held 71 rounds. After two days of winning my comrades' confidence, I was issued a gendarme's carbine—a reliable Mauser-style bolt-action rifle with a five-round magazine—and 128 eight-millimeter rounds of ammunition. A quarter of my rounds were tracers, because if we had to shoot, it would most likely be in darkness or fog. I was very proud of that gun! I carved my warrior name into the wooden buttstock: *Pomsta*, which means "vengeance" in Slovak.

The rest of the squad had a real hodgepodge of weaponry, including WWI vintage six-shooters, standard-issue Slovak Army rifles, and plenty of hand grenades. In the beginning, we also carried a massive Russian 14.5-millimeter bolt-action anti-tank rifle with about a fifty-inch barrel. It took two men to carry this monster (which proved inconvenient during our clandestine cross-country marches), so we ultimately abandoned it at headquarters. As our principal mission was demolition, our primary ordnance comprised satchels containing ten-kilogram steel boxes packed with TNT as well as a supply of blasting caps and several yards of detonation cord.

Life with the *Partizáns*

During September and for most of October, we had plenty of food. We ate mostly spiced pork stew with beans, cabbage, and potatoes. When back at our base camp, we received rations of alcohol, cigarettes, and excellent peasant bread. I always traded the cigarettes for bread. The food was either purchased or appropriated from the local folk. Later, when we were driven out of the villages, our rations shrank; a dire situation—especially during the long marches in snow. Even then, starving men were willing to exchange bread for cigarettes, a senseless bargain that led to my lifetime aversion to smoking.

On Saturday, everybody got a shave. My "beard" was viewed with derision, but Batko ruled that since I would probably be killed soon anyway, I might as well be presentable. When our leader found out that Milos had never "been with a woman," the entire squad chipped in to pay a more-than-willing local widow to do the honors while we stood guard to make sure that none of her relatives interfered. I was offered the same privileges but I was too scared, and besides, at this time I was unable to keep my food down; my intestines were full of little white worms I must have picked up from the pork I had eaten back in September.

Otherwise, I remember the period until the end of October 1944 as reasonably happy and sufficiently busy to take my mind off the fate of my family. The days were warm, but the nights were cold. Frost and snow arrived in the first week of November and continued through to the liberation—it was one of the most severe winters in recent memory. When deep snow settled along the mountaintops and in the valleys, we could move only along paths we hoped were inaccessible to German patrols. During this treacherous winter, our losses came not so much from bullets as from exposure to the elements.

Rules of Engagement

Ironically, belonging to the mining squad surely saved my life. We were under orders to stay out of villages; to relocate our campsite every few days; to spend most of the time moving from one attack position to another; to leave our wounded behind; to avoid firefights at all cost; to retreat when confronted by any force; never to steal food from the peasants; and to always pay cash for services rendered by the locals (we always had more than enough Slovak state crowns to pay our way). Our makeshift rules dictated that we sleep in hayricks instead of enjoying the greater comfort of the farmhouses, that we arrive at attack sites at sunset, and that we execute our missions during the hours of darkness if at all possible.

I was surprised by the amount of paperwork that was necessary to keep track of what we were doing. Every time our ragtag group showed up at another *partizán* base or when the chain of command changed (which was often), we were required to submit paperwork explaining who we were and where we came from. As I understood it, this was a requirement imposed by the newly formed regular Czechoslovak Army that believed only through careful bookkeeping could we substantiate our claim to be a properly organized military force. Ivanov, our commissar, had to sign off on these manning lists—payroll was the alleged purpose of such detailed tallies, but I think it was just a way of keeping tabs on us. However, we were in fact occasionally paid in Slovak currency. Tato grumbled about such bureaucracy, because if any of us was taken prisoner and one of these lists happened to land in the enemy's hands (which was quite likely), it would be our death warrant. Cursing profusely, Batko also made it clear that in his opinion all this record-keeping was an idiotic drill perpetrated by regular army officers intent on imposing order on chaos, when deliberate disorder would have been the best way to maintain security.

Demo Man

When I first met Batko, he was just coming from a sortie that had to be aborted because his guerilla fighters were not familiar with the Trenčín territory. My escape from Trenčín and the exaggerated story of how I hijacked a Bren gun with a hand grenade impressed the *partizán* leader, and Batko decided I was just the right sort of decoy to place at the head of the next raid.

The next attack on the dual-track Trenčín-Žilina railroad line was ordered immediately after the squad returned to brigade headquarters. This rail line was of strategic importance, because it facilitated the rapid transfer of troop reinforcements from the south to the north and vice versa, while the Soviets did their best to keep the Germans guessing about where the main thrust of the fall offensive would be aimed.

The objective was to find a curve on the railroad where the wheels of the engine would be pressing hard on the inside of the track and pick just the right moment to set off the explosives. Ideally, the locomotive would initiate a fuse that in turn set off the TNT charge that would sever one of the rails. If done correctly, the locomotive would derail and plunge down the railroad embankment, hauling the rest of the cars with it.

I was now to be a "demo man." My entire military training took perhaps not more than half an hour. A wooden plank was used as a blackboard to explain how to blow a rail track so that it breaks at just the right time. I was to accompany Batko, who carried three metal boxes of TNT. This explosive has a waxy consistency and is essentially inert—it only explodes when set off by a fuse or blasting cap. My job was to pass three thin copper tubes about three inches long to Batko, along with some strips of surgical tape to secure the fuses to the outside flange of the rail. These tubes contained a small amount of an explosive that ignited when struck by even a light force. Other members of the squad spread out and took positions that allowed them to provide cover fire for us in case of pursuit or if we were discovered prematurely.

And so began my first mission against the Germans, establishing a pattern that was to be repeated many times in the days to come.

War!

The squad quietly approached the ambush site, which was near the village of Opatova. We moved with great stealth because the villages were full of informers. By that time, the hills surrounding Trenčín were declared to be a "free fire zone"—the Germans and their henchmen could shoot on sight anyone found wandering through the woods. That's why we kept off roads and even the footpaths. Sometimes I had to walk ahead of the squad, because I knew the area. In addition to my rifle, I also had two hand grenades dangling from my belt, some leather pouches with ammunition clips, and a rucksack with my food and the all-important half of a standard army-issue shelter—the infamous "pup tent." The squad alternated in carrying the heavy satchels bearing the explosives.

At that time the moon was shining brightly, so we marched all night and slept during the day. Progress was slow. The second night, it started raining lightly. It was very dark. Late in the evening, we arrived at the edge of the embankment overlooking the twin sets of rails. We wrapped ourselves in our tent-halves and tried to keep dry.

There was not much traffic on the rail line below us or on the highway running parallel to it. A few passenger trains sped by, then we heard our quarry approaching—a freight train rumbling along from the south. Its labored, puffing cadence told us it was pulling a heavy load. Batko was pleased; conditions were ideal for our mission. The freight train could be heard from a good distance, and we figured we had about nine minutes to booby-trap a rail on the northbound tracks.

Following a proven tactic, we set up two flanking positions of two men each, spread about a hundred yards apart. The mine-laying crew—three of us—then proceeded to place the explosives and arm them. The trick was to cause the locomotive to set off the explosion with its forward wheels. This was accomplished by taping the blasting caps to the rail in the proper location. When the wheel smashed the cap, it set the detonation cord burning at a rate of one foot per second; when the burning det cord reached the primary charge, it ignited a second blasting cap inserted into the TNT. It took skill and experience to calculate the perfect length of det cord to ensure that the explosion occurred precisely beneath the heaviest part of the train, which was the engine tender filled with water and coal.

The flat ground separating the edge of the forest from the railroad was freshly plowed and very muddy. There were only two walking paths between the adjoining fields. We moved into position in a ditch at the foot of the embankment. We could hear the train approaching—it was very close. The light rain muffled the sound. We now had less than five minutes to lay our deadly trap. I climbed up to the rails and squatted there watching the headlights of the locomotive as it crept nearer. Batko excavated some of the stone ballast from between the railroad ties and nested two boxes of TNT under the rails. They were fused in such a way that at least one was sure to go off.

Batko now called for the blasting caps he would attach to the detonation cords and tape to the rail. I was carrying these sensitive explosive devices in a thick leather pouch designed for the purpose; it was lined with soft cotton padding to cushion the caps. In the excitement of passing Batko the caps, I failed to snap the lid securely shut and all of the dangerous little tubes—perhaps a dozen—spilled out on the ground when I jumped up to follow Batko away from the tracks.

This was a critical error, because the squad had no way of replacing these extremely scarce detonators, even though we had plenty of TNT. As Batko was high-tailing it back to the edge of the forest, the lights from the engine illuminated enough of the roadbed so that I could actually see the slim, copper detonation cylinders on the ground, so I scooped them up.

Frantically shoving them into my pocket, I grabbed my rifle and started running for all I was worth. In an unthinking panic, I made a second horrible mistake. In retracing my steps to the tracks, I found myself on the edge of the muddy fields instead of the firm path that ran between them. In my confusion and haste, I could not locate the path.

Imagine sprinting for your life through a sticky paste—it was like a bad dream. After about twenty-five meters I knew I had better hit the ground, because the locomotive was passing the spot where we had placed the explosives—right behind my back. As I collapsed face-first in the ooze, the TNT charges erupted with an ear-splitting blast that sounded like the world was coming to an end. Shards of jagged iron whizzed past me; I heard them sizzling as they plowed into the mud all around. I looked back and saw the locomotive slowly roll off the embankment like some mortally wounded dinosaur, and it was heading straight for me! I could hear the cries of the occupants of the train and the crunching of metal and wood as cars jackknifed down the line and the wreckage piled up across the rails.

By some miracle, I was not hit by the flying shrapnel that used to be a train, but I did get slightly scalded by the hot water and steam escaping from the ruptured boiler. I hauled myself to my feet and started running again when I heard a shot followed by a strange *whooshing* sound. I saw a white light arcing over me, leaving a comet-like trail that exploded into a slowly descending bright flame. The German guards on the train were sending up illumination flares. I hit the ground again, hoping I hadn't been seen. Tracer bullets from a machine gun flew overhead, raking the edge of the forest. When the first flare burned out, I got up and kept running, my heart pounding in my ears. In a few moments, another flare lit the sky, and again I dropped and laid still. This cycle was repeated several times, allowing me to advance incrementally across the sodden field. Why nobody saw me remains a mystery to me, except that I was probably indistinguishable from a lump of mud when I hit the ground. Tracers continued to fly all over the landscape, but by concentrating their fire on the edge of the forest, the gunners were shooting too high.

It was my good fortune that they apparently only had one flare gun on the train, so it took them a few precious seconds to reload. Whenever they shot up a flare, I could hear a pop before the flare started climbing.

It took about three seconds for the flare to reach the apex of its trajectory, and then a small parachute deployed that enabled the bright light to descend slowly. Whenever I heard that telltale *pop*, I just flattened myself into the muck, and prayed that the machine gunners would not see me. Luckily, they were too busy watching the distant wood line.

The guards must have been green recruits. During the intervals between the illumination from the flares, the gunners wasted their ammunition by shooting too high to hit anything. Even with the tracers to help them, they were firing blindly—their bursts were not aimed at all. The gunners were on a flat car well up the embankment, making it difficult for them to rake the field at a lethal waist-high level.

Our squad of guerilla raiders finally regrouped at the edge of the forest, including the third member of the mine-laying crew. Nobody was injured. Everyone felt heroic, having seriously damaged the entire front end of a freight train that turned out to be carrying soldiers and their equipment.[1] Most of the damage was a result of the derailment of the locomotive and the tender rather than the explosion itself. It would take only about half a day for the Slovak maintenance engineers to get the tracks cleared and repaired, but from a *partizán* perspective, that was considered to be a victory, as such surprise attacks by an unseen enemy were very hard on morale.

There were other times when we repeated pretty much the same drill but did not end up so lucky. In the absence of reliable intelligence about train schedules, there was no way of knowing for sure what we were going to blow up once we armed the explosives. Our only consolation was that any wreck blocked rail traffic on a strategic line and crippled the transportation system that sustained the German field force.

My "Execution"

In the wake of our raid, we withdrew over a small hill where the random firing from the train couldn't reach us, and Batko checked the

---

[1]This event is also noted on p. 332 of the comprehensive History of Partizáns in Czechoslovakia, 1941–45, published in Slovak by the PRAVDA Publishing Organization in Bratislava, 1984.

readiness of everyone's weapons in case we were ambushed at the next road crossing. He had apparently seen me spill the precious caps into the mud, as he drew his revolver and said that he would now get rid of the Jewish kid who lost his detonator caps. Shoving my hand into my trouser pocket, I produced a fistful of the mud-encrusted copper cylinders with a grin. The entire squad backed away in horror. I completely forgot that even slight squeezing of the caps or landing hard on a stone would have caused them to explode. Each cap contained enough explosive to blow a hole in my side. By some miracle, none of them detonated. The waterlogged field over which I hopped must have cushioned my fall. Fortunately, there were no stones on the ground—I guess that farmer was proud of his fine fields!

Later I was told that Batko was only joking when he threatened to execute me, but I am still not sure, having witnessed incidents that revealed how the Soviets enforced discipline.

That's how I became an expert in the derailing of trains; it was my baptism of fire, and also my initiation into the ranks of the *partizáns*. I had proven myself worthy of their trust. I would be using these skills again as we launched raids farther up the Váh river valley, and later during the long march east.

Shortly afterwards, our little squad was assigned to a new area commander, a Ukrainian captain by the name of Bohinski. The man was a beast, although he was always smiling as he ordered men into suicide missions.

We just kept moving in the northerly direction along the railroad to find places where the tracks were sufficiently close to the edge of a forest to provide cover for our operations. As time passed, the raids became more difficult, because the Germans now placed a machine gun nest on a flat car that was pushed ahead of the engine. There was at least one case in which hostages were taken from a village near our ambush site. That made it impossible to depend on the locals for food and support. It also increased the chance of mobile SS troops being called in to hunt us down as we slipped away from our work of devastation. In the days to come, I experienced many close calls but nothing in my entire *partizán* service ever approached the thrill and excellent results of that first raid at Opatova. I suppose it was a case of "beginner's luck."

The Way of the *Partizán*

I came to admire the Batko's cool professionalism in all operational matters. Until we lost him (under incredibly stupid circumstances) we never suffered enemy-caused casualties. Perhaps the main problem with the later attempts by the insurgent Slovak army to shift to *partizán* warfare was the lack of combat know-how to employ improvised tactics. Regular army officers did not trust our motley band to stand up to the Germans. I am convinced that if the uprising had been planned and conducted as a joint regular–*partizán* operation, its military impact on the Allied war effort would have been far greater and the casualties lower. The Slovak staff officers in charge of the uprising were suspicious of our irregular and uncoordinated methods, but the military situation in the fall of 1944 made our ragtag guerilla outfit vastly more effective than most regular army units. We delivered good results for very little cost in casualties and materiel.

Batko's training saved my life many times. For instance, he constantly reminded us that immobile objects are hard to identify at night, even when illuminated; in low light, the enemy would first only see moving objects. Raking the surrounding area with machine-gun fire following one of our attacks (a common German tactic) was intended to scare us into movement, so we would become easy targets. Batko's advice was to freeze, even if under fire, and move only after the enemy has determined that the *partizáns* had disappeared. It takes nerves of steel not to run when a machine gun is firing at you!

Later, I came to appreciate the utility of this rule, especially when standing guard. The trick for a sentry was to stand perfectly still, so as not to be noticed and eliminated. In winter, it was impossible for a sentry to remain immobile; the bone-numbing cold made anyone on guard duty stomp his feet and hop around to keep warm. The Russians as well as the SS had snipers who could take out a sentry in darkness, illuminated only by starlight. During brilliantly clear moonlit nights one could easily detect the silhouette of a sentry in motion from long distances. I always made sure to find a position where the bright moon projected no shadow against the snow.

False Start

Our method of operation was vastly different from what was being practiced in the liberated territories around Banská Bystrica, the epicenter of the uprising. Corralled in this mountain fastness was a mixed bag of refugees: most of the Jews who were still left in Slovakia, everyone who declared themselves anti-Nazis, escaped prisoners (both POWs and those of the criminal sort), and the Slovak Army deserters. Following Soviet political doctrine, the liberated territory was set up as a military enclave, which at the point of maximum expansion encompassed an area of about 8,000 square miles of mostly mountainous countryside. The army was responsible for providing security for this area while the politicians set up the Czechoslovak Republic, a task that was taking place 300 miles away from the front lines.

The rechristened 1st Czechoslovak Army, now recognized as an Allied force, had orders to employ conventional defensive military tactics while the Soviets attempted to advance through the passes in the Carpathian Mountains to lend support. The liberated area quickly assumed the outward manifestations of an organized state—there was a legislature, a judiciary, a lively press corps, several radio stations, a military staff, railway-mounted artillery, and a liaison team from the OSS (Office of Strategic Services, predecessor of the CIA). Delegations from London and Moscow were flown in and put up in local hotels. American B-17 bombers based in Italy airlifted in arms and military advisors. For their part, the Russians brought in two battalions of Slovaks from Kiev, soldiers who had defected to the Soviets in 1942 and been trained in conventional warfare, Russian style.

Meanwhile, the Communist Party (claiming a leadership role because of the prospects of overall liberation by the Soviets) dominated the debate over military strategy with the representatives of the Slovak officer corps that was loyal to the London-exiled government. Looking back at the brief nine-week lifespan of the liberated territories, I find the pretenses of an organized government a laughable tragedy. Instead of preparing for the inevitable, the dueling functionaries wasted time maneuvering for power and prestige.

On October 28, elite German divisions steamrolled over the liberated territory. There followed a period of widespread executions and deportations of mutinous Slovak soldiers and removal to death camps for the Jews. Ditches that had been dug to stop German panzers would soon be filled with the victims of mass executions. Had I gone with Kartal to join the insurrectionist elements of the regular Slovak Army instead of hitching my star to Batko's *partizán* band, I might well have ended up in one of those mass graves. My instincts served me well. Our loosely organized and quite undisciplined squad of miners, clothed in a motley array of civilian garments and wandering undetected from ambush to ambush, had more of a chance of survival than the uniformed army.

The regular army spent more time trying to figure out the latest political rearrangements than in fighting. The army command apparently would not (or could not) admit that the uprising was doomed from its inception. When orders were finally issued in late October to disperse into the mountains and continue resistance by means of *partizán* warfare, it was too late. The army had no pre-positioned bases in the mountains. It had no formal plans about how to execute such a major shift in tactics. Only the Soviet *partizán* command had the forethought and organization to establish well-provisioned hideouts to which its units could retreat.

"Batko's Miners" avoided most of the calamities that befell the 1st Czechoslovak Army. Our squad was never hit by artillery or bombs. We avoided roads where we might encounter German motorized infantry. We learned how to carry our own supplies and live off the land. And after a while, there were no more informers among us who could betray our location. Our leaders knew where the pre-positioned caches were located, so we could always fade into the hills and survive, even in an extremely cold winter that made the conventional forces throw up their hands in surrender.

EXPERIENCES

From the time I joined the *partizáns* until we were ordered into winter quarters, most of our time was spent moving to and from suitable ambush sites. My memory is now a bit fuzzy about how often we did that—there were at least four missions after Opatova—but I can still vividly recall some of the episodes on the way to and from these raids.

The Roadblock

At that time, the *partizán* brigade command was located in the ruins of a castle at Uhrovec. Upon returning from a train-derailing mission near Dubnica, we received instructions to block a nearby road to prevent access by German motorized patrols. This was normally accomplished by felling a large tree on a blind curve using several well-placed sticks of dynamite. Then we would hide one or two antitank mines among the branches to complicate removal of the obstacle. The trick was to camouflage the mines under the leaves and string tripwires from the needle-plunger detonator mechanism through the branches of the fallen tree. When done, somebody had to crawl in among the branches and carefully remove the cotter pin safety from beneath the plunger. Batko was an old hand at this.

A suitable oak tree was located and felled, and the mines were artfully placed. I helped string the all-important tripwires. After that, I carefully extricated myself and crawled back to the roadway. As we were walking back to where we had previously set up a defensive position, a dispatch rider roared up on a motorcycle. It seems there was another *partizán* group coming down the road escorting a convoy of food and supplies, and we were ordered to immediately remove the trap we had just set.

After suffering a long stream of Batko's colorful invective, we trudged back to the tree, set up another defensive position and slowly, *very slowly,* threaded the two safety pins back into the tiny holes separating the spring-loaded plungers from the detonation caps. We then departed, leaving the job of removing the huge tree from the roadway to our comrades who needed to pass. It was a kind of practical joke, as we knew they could not be sure we had thoroughly de-armed the booby-trap.

The brigade command did not thank us for that. We were reprimanded (with a smile) for "poor *partizán* discipline," even though we had performed the very dangerous job of laying the antitank mines and then removing them. Anyway, the entire incident enhanced our reputation as skillful operators.

The Banovce Ambush

After another raid on the railroad in mid-October, we were scurrying back to our base camp as usual. There was always a possibility that the Germans or the Hlinka Guard would dispatch trucks full of troops to intercept us as we crossed highways, which we often did without much cover. Our method was to walk as long as possible along the edge of a forest then dash across the open land, dangerously exposed until we could reach another cluster of trees on the opposite side.

We started to relax a bit and let our guard down when we finally reached what we believed to be *partizán*-occupied territory near our base. We were walking along a cow path behind a hedgerow that blocked visibility from a highway that ran beneath us in a valley. Suddenly, there was an eruption of small arms fire on the roadway below. It was accompanied by shouting and cries of men who had been hit. An officer wearing Czechoslovak Army insignia suddenly appeared and ordered us to deploy on the highway to block the escape of a fleeing Hlinka Guard detachment his men had just ambushed.

There were two truckloads of the hated black-shirted Hlinka Guard troops headed for Prievidza in the direction of our brigade HQ. A mixed *partizán* and Czechoslovak Army group had set up firing positions across the valley and intercepted the Guards' convoy. The enemy responded by establishing a defensive perimeter in the ditches that ran along the roadway—and they were taking casualties.

From where we were located we could look directly down on the Guards hugging the roadside. They were firing back on their attackers across the valley and had no idea of our presence—they were sitting ducks. Tato set up our light machine gun and we opened up on them; he emptied all of his magazines into the Guards who were now caught in a crossfire. I squeezed off the five rounds from the clip in my bolt-action rifle in the general direction of the black uniforms although in the confusion of the firefight, I had no way of knowing if I hit anyone. At that point, some of the Guards fled while others threw up their hands in surrender. I saw a number of men in black uniforms lying motionless. Tato then took all of my surplus ammunition to reload his magazine to give the Guards a parting fusillade. By the time he had fully reloaded, there were no more targets to shoot at. The fact that both Tato and I ran out of ammunition reflected our special operations mission: We were essentially a clandestine demo team, so we carried a lot of explosives and basic survival gear, but very little small arms ammunition—we avoided firefights at all cost.

At this point, our squad emerged from cover and pursued the retreating Guards who had vanished around a turn in the road. As a unit strictly dedicated to mining, we were prohibited from such aggressive action. I lost one of my ill-fitting shoes as I ran, but did not notice it at the time. Although bullets kept whizzing all around, I moved as fast as I could until I was flagged down on the roadway by a Russian soldier whom I knew. He ordered me to help him carry a wounded Russian officer to seek medical attention. As it turned out, the officer was one of the original paratroopers, and a very popular fellow. We made an improvised stretcher out of his green military coat and tried to lift the wounded man. I was horrified. His entire back was one huge gaping hole, with gore and ragged pieces of his lungs hanging out and gurgling as he bled profusely. All I could do was to take a piece of his shirt and stuff it into the hole. We had to move quickly because German armored cars would likely be arriving any moment to relieve the badly mauled Hlinka Guards.

We hauled the wounded man up the hill and put him down. He was dead. An elaborate military funeral was held for him the next day, and I was recognized for my assistance. They said I was the kid who came to the officer's aid in a hail of bullets—and had my shoe shot off for my trouble. It's a good story, anyway …

Our squad was reprimanded again by the brigade commissar for getting involved in what he labeled as a poorly executed ambush. We had expended so much ammunition shooting at the Hlinka Guards that we were left without adequate firepower to protect ourselves in case we had been attacked later. Batko was scolded for yet another example of his lack of "*partizán* discipline."

A Bungled Ambush

Following several close calls we had while moving to and from our raids, Batko decided we would hide during daylight and walk only during nights. This could be only accomplished with the aid of moonlight; on cloudy nights or when it rained, our progress was very slow.

Late in October, we were returning from what I believe was our last raid on the Trenčín-Žilina rail line. It was a miserable night. Pelted by a steady freezing rain, we were soaked to the skin. My new military coat was made out of a thick felt, and it became heavy and smelly. The area in which we could freely operate had shrunk to a few villages in the mountains. The former luxury of getting ferried by truck to and from our jumping-off points for our raids was long gone. The German and Hlinka Guard patrol cars were masters of the roads.

One night, after a good deal of busting brush traipsing cross-country, Batko shifted our route to the roads, as we would otherwise never make it back to our base before daylight. It must have been after midnight when we heard the grinding gears of a truck coming up the hill ahead of us. Batko had an idea: Capturing a truck would solve our transportation dilemma. Well seasoned in ambush techniques, we instinctively took up positions behind trees, flipped off the safety on our weapons and got ready to lob hand grenades into the back of the truck. It was Tato's job to take out the driver and anyone else in the cab.

As the truck crawled up the road by the dim illumination provided by its blackout headlights, our lead man tossed a concussion grenade onto the roof. We heard it land, but it failed to detonate. We could clearly hear a great deal of cursing in Russian coming from the cab, so we suspended the attack. The occupants of the truck turned out to be *partizáns* being ferried to another location! Fortunately, no one was hurt, and Batko was called before the division commissar for yet another tongue-lashing.

Back in camp, others poked fun at our trigger-happy band, which had already earned a reputation for practicing unconventional warfare with high explosives. We were teased mercilessly for our incompetence; we couldn't even get a hand grenade to work properly.

Failure of the Uprising

At the end of October, eight Axis divisions (including four crack SS divisions and one pro-Nazi Slovak division) were withdrawn from Poland to suppress the uprising. With clinical precision, the Germans and their Slovak collaborators overwhelmed the militarily untenable position of the 1st Czechoslovak Army around Banská Bystrica. After neutralizing the Czechoslovak forces, the Germans and their allies had ample military resources to pursue the Soviet-led *partizáns* that had been operating with little interference from mountain bases or relatively inaccessible settlements. The troops attacking us were mostly former prisoners of war, the so-called "Vlasov soldiers," after the Ukrainian general who commanded anti-Soviet fighters.[2] These men had expected that, after the Germans' victory, they would end up in positions of power in the Ukraine, Byelorussia, Lithuania, and Estonia.

---

[2]Andrei Andreyevich Vlasov was a highly decorated Soviet general who, following his capture in the summer of 1942, came to the conclusion that Stalin and the Bolsheviks were the true enemies of the Russian people. He was courted by the Germans to lead an anti-Soviet element within the German Army comprised largely of Soviet Army POWs and anti-Communist refugees (Vlasov, it should be noted, was not anti-Semitic). A charismatic figure, Vlasov attracted thousands of volunteers and pushed for the formation of a Russian Liberation Army under the aegis of the Wehrmacht. Hitler never trusted him and the organization existed in name only to be used as a propaganda tool. Russian (and other Eastern ethnic) divisions within the Wehrmacht were consolidated and transferred to Himmler's SS in September of 1944. After the war, Vlasov was tried as a traitor and hanged in Moscow. Whether he was a genuine anti-Soviet Russian nationalist or simply an opportunist is still debated by historians.

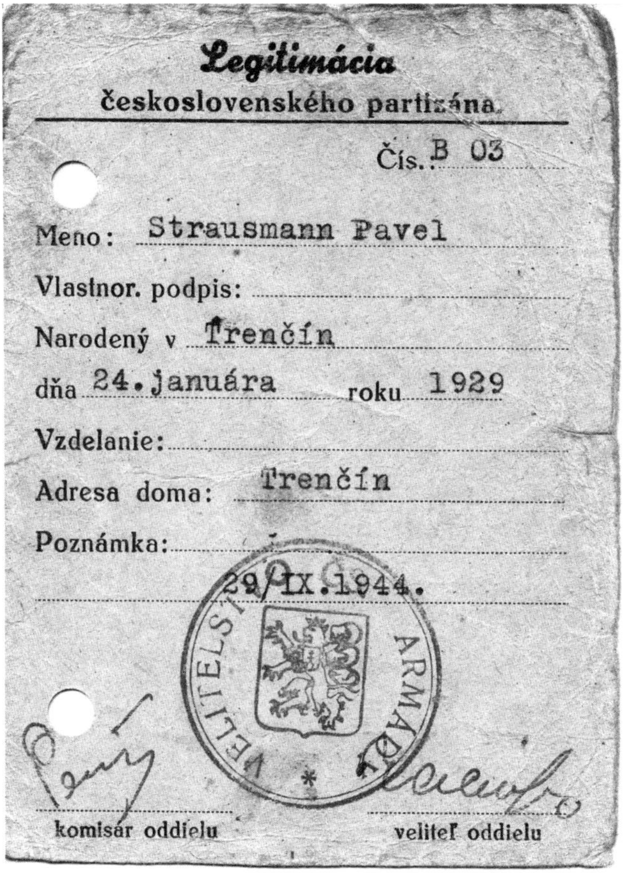
Legitimácia
československého partizána
Čís. B 03
Meno: Strausmann Pavel
Vlastnor. podpis:
Narodený v Trenčín
dňa 24. januára roku 1929
Vzdelanie:
Adresa doma: Trenčín
Poznámka:
29/IX.1944.
komisár oddielu veliteľ oddielu

3. *Partizán* Identity Card

Vlasov's men had joined the Germans in 1941 and 1942, when putting on an SS uniform seemed preferable to ending up in a German slave labor camp. German officers commanded these troops above the battalion level. The SS commanders viewed these auxiliary forces (called "police action groups") as goon squads, ideal for doing their dirty work—such as burning villages, executing hostages, and rooting out Jews and *partizáns*. In occupied lands, they employed extreme violence against civilians including torture, wanton murder, and mass executions. Their specialty was the suppression of "bandits," which meant hunting us, even in remote places where regular German troops would never care to go.[3]

As the end of the war approached, many of these non-German SS soldiers sought refuge among the *partizán* units by claiming to be runaways from prisoner-of-war camps. Since most of the Slovak *partizán* groups were shattered after the collapse of the uprising, it was often impossible to distinguish whether a small group of men approaching you in the forest was an SS reconnaissance team, remnants of a broken-up *partizán* brigade, or a few ex-Vlasov operatives pretending to be anti-Nazi fighters.

Throughout this period, I became keenly aware that misidentification of who was a partizán and who was not could mean the difference between life and death. Most of the partizáns had destroyed all of their identification papers, which could have marked them for summary execution if captured. I retained my partizán identification papers throughout the entire ordeal. The papers were officially stamped as having been issued by the 1st Czechoslovak Army on September 29, 1944. As added insurance, I always carried a hand grenade in my clothing, even—no, especially—while sleeping.

Losing Batko

I certainly owe my life to the wisdom and survival know-how of Batko, who somehow managed to mold a motley collection of individuals into a team that functioned effectively. Although I cannot say for sure where I got this story, I heard that Batko was allowed to parachute into Slovakia and operate as a *partizán* as an alternative to a death sentence. I do not recall what his alleged offense was. That was a frequent case with many Soviet *partizáns* who had originally avoided capture by the advancing German armies in 1941. Instead of being killed by the Germans or their own commissars (who shot retreating soldiers), a few of these survival-

---

[3]Based on Strassmann's unsavory description, it would appear that these "Vlasov soldiers" might have been the remnants of the notorious SS Waffen-Sturm-Brigade RONA (aka "Kaminski Brigade") which were incorporated into Vlasov's token command in the fall of 1944. The Kaminski Brigade had been employed as an auxiliary anti-partisan force since 1941 and garnered a reputation for looting, atrocities and sundry war crimes.

ists retreated into the woods and marshes of Byelorussia, from where they waged effective *partizán* warfare for almost three years. When the Russian front advanced into Poland, these *partizáns* were brought before the NKVD (the Soviet political discipline enforcers). Anyone who espoused nationalist or independent views, or was suspected of being an anti-Soviet fighter was either executed or sentenced to hard labor in Siberia.

Batko was lucky. He lost his left hand in combat (I suspect it was blown off by the premature detonation of a blasting cap). That earned him a new lease on life, as he was allowed to become a *partizán* warrior. Even though he was never fully accepted as one of the officers who were welcome at brigade HQ, Batko was respected for his reckless courage. That's why he was given the unenviable task of leading the mining squad, certainly one of the most dangerous assignments in *partizán* warfare.

As early November set in, the members of our team, which never exceeded twelve men, were getting physically exhausted and quite sick. The skin on our feet became infected, which made walking increasingly painful. I could not hold down our food rations of bread and fried bacon. We had not washed for a while, and, while sleeping in haystacks, we all picked up lice and fleas. For a while, I did not have a good coat, since half of it was burned one night while I fell asleep too close to the embers of a campfire.

It was around this time that we lost Tato and Milos. Both were wounded and left in one of the villages we passed through, never to be heard from again. After the war, I was unable to locate either of them. A few Slovak members of our squad disappeared without explanation—we suspected they saw the end coming and were looking for opportunities to slip away. They were replaced by a gypsy, a Ukrainian (who claimed to have escaped from a prison train), and three Jews, including old Mr. Kolin, a WWI veteran close to sixty years old. We had our doubts about how useful such an old man might be, but he won us over with his ingratiating personality and sage advice. He refused to carry a gun, but just tagged along as we marched. Like some mongrel pup, he refused to leave us—and he became more of a father figure than a commando. Ultimately, he took charge of increasingly touchy negotiations with villagers about food and other supplies, and he had imaginative ways of solving everyday small household problems. Batko—an old softy under his coarse exterior—did not have the heart to cast him out to face certain death.

Amazingly, old Kolin survived the tribulations of *partizán* existence after the fall of the uprising. I have no idea how he could possibly have done that. After the war, he came to visit me. It turned out that he was a remote relative of my sister's future husband. And so it is a small world.

One day as the winter was approaching, we were sent on a foraging mission to gather supplies to be cached in one of our hideouts. Our practice of always staying off the roads and keeping to the edge of the woods did not do us much good on this occasion. The leaves had already fallen, and the countryside was barren and bleak, making it difficult to find cover during our marches.

It was not far from Zavada that we spied a truck approaching us at high speed. We all took whatever cover we could find, except that crazy Batko, who (with his usual swagger) kept walking calmly down the center of the road, with his PPSh submachine gun slung over his gimpy left arm. A machine gun mounted on top of the truck cab started firing at him, but instead of leaping out of the road, Batko started running straight at the truck while firing bursts from his weapon. Batko was cut down instantly. We managed to fire a few rounds at the truck as it reversed direction and disappeared around a curve in the road. To this day, I do not know whether Batko's suicidal actions were calculated to destroy the truck or to give his squad time to get away—or both.

Uprising Statistics

The key events in the abortive Slovak National Uprising, now glorified as a "heroic liberation movement," can be summarized as follows:

August 28, 1944: Uprising begins

September 1, 1944: Germans disarm Eastern Slovak Army Command. The original battle plan is doomed.

September 6, 1944: The liberated Czechoslovak area declares its independence and announces the formation of a new government to rule the occupied territory.

October 28, 1944: Organized uprising suppressed; most of the insurrectionist Slovak forces disband and the men return to their villages to lay low.

October 28, 1944 – April 5, 1945: Insurgency continued by *partizáns* in small groups or teams. Russians, Jews, Communists, and those Slovaks identified as leaders of the uprising remain in hiding during the winter under conditions of extreme duress.

The rapid demise of the uprising should not be seen as only a marginal disturbance; consider these statistics:

Slovak Army + Volunteers at start = 60,000

Partizán battalions when uprising faltered = 18,000

German troops employed to suppress the uprising = 40,000

Hlinka Guards loyal to Nazis = 20,000

STORIES

The Soviet commanders applied brutal discipline to enforce security and political objectives as well as control through intimidation. I recall a Soviet sniper, an officer, who was conspicuous for carrying a silencer attached to his semiautomatic SVT-40 Tokarev rifle—even while on duty at the headquarters. It turned out this man was an enforcer and executioner. I witnessed one summary court martial of an escaped prisoner from a German camp who was accused of trying to infiltrate our ranks. He was led away by two men and followed by our ever-present officer with the silencer mounted on the muzzle of his rifle. A short while later only three men returned.

My first encounter with the severity of Soviet discipline occurred at a campfire late one night. That afternoon we stopped a moving van transporting someone's household belongings. We searched the contents for suitable items of clothing we could commandeer, such as underwear or waterproof outerwear. In a bureau drawer, somebody found a pre-WWI vintage revolver that was rusted with disuse but still loaded. Since all of the members of our squad already had side arms, I was presented with the revolver; it would be of little use except to dispatch myself in the event of capture. At the campfire, I was cleaning the weapon when it went off. The bullet whizzed over everybody's heads. The commissar came over and announced that this was my lucky day. If anyone had been wounded, he advised in all seriousness, I would have been executed on the spot. The revolver was confiscated and smashed with rocks.

Soviet Discipline

One of the saddest episodes from the history of the uprising concerns the fate of the Nováky battalion. This unit was formed from a group of young Jewish men (and a few women) who had been liberated from the Nováky labor camp during the revolt. Despite having no training and inadequate armament and leadership, the outfit was thrown into the battle line, where it was immediately set upon by veteran German mechanized infantry and armored troops in a well-coordinated assault. Of course the Germans routed the Nováky battalion, which sustained high casualties. Those who survived the ordeal were turned over to the Soviet *partizán* command, which was seeking trustworthy recruits to bolster its ranks.

En route to their new assignment, the Nováky fighters passed through a village. As was the general practice, they stopped for a rest and went in search of food from the locals. One of the men leaned his rifle against the doorpost as he entered a peasant's cottage. As it was later related to me, our *partizán* commander, the dreaded Captain Bohinski, happened by. When he saw the rifle leaning against the door, Bohinski was furious. The entire group was summoned and informed that a *partizán* may *never* leave his weapon unattended. Although this rule was generally understood, it wasn't taken too seriously. But Captain Bohinski took it seriously. To set an example, he ordered the offending soldier to be summarily executed.

This episode (in slightly varying versions) was widely discussed in our dugouts. Since Bohinski had inspected our team on two occasions, we were well aware that even the fearless Batko was afraid of him. Captain Bohinski, too, was quite conscious of the effect he had on the men; he was always impeccably attired in a tailored leather jacket and leather pants, with medals covering the breast of his overcoat. We thought he was a jackass, but a rather dangerous one.

Some time in January, during the retreat from a raiding party, we were the target of a mortar attack and Bohinski was wounded. Though the *partizán* rule was to leave our wounded behind, in the case of Captain Bohinski we were ordered to make a stretcher and carry him through hip-deep snow up a steep mountain face. We would rather have left him behind.

Close Call in Lužna

Terror was also used to keep the villagers in line, although nowadays many receive generous pensions for services rendered in the uprising and are unwilling to talk about it. In February 1945, I found temporary shelter in the village of Liptovska Lužna. I had been sent there as a punishment (which I will discuss later). I was instructed to look up an innkeeper who had a reputation for harboring *partizáns* in need of a warm bed and decent food while recovering from wounds or illness. One day the innkeeper's sister-in-law came running out to the shed where I was sleeping, pleading for my help because there were *partizáns* at the door demanding money. When I boldly confronted the band, it was obvious I had made a terrible mistake.

This was apparently one of the many gangs of ruffians who were rampaging through the countryside towards the end of the war. Some were escaped criminals seeking legitimacy as "freedom fighters," others were turncoat Nazi mercenaries who tried to save their hides by tagging on to one of the many *partizán* groups roaming the hills. On the way, they were raping and killing. They lived off the land and intimidated the terrified peasantry.

The leader of the gang marched me out in front of a few assembled villagers and announced that I would be shot for interfering with the collection of essential supplies for the *partizáns*. My hands were tied behind my back and I was led down the steps to the river (the customary execution grounds) while the villagers watched in silence. It looked to me that this would surely be my end.

At this moment coming up the road was a tall man I only knew as Lieutenant Rudo. He was an ethnic German Communist who had seen me a few times while I was serving as a sentry at headquarters. I can still remember Rudo's unusual weapon: Towards the end of the war, some SS units were supplied with a prototype rapid-fire large-caliber machine pistol made in Austria by Heckler and Koch. These weapons looked and functioned very much like the AK-47 assault rifle adopted by the Soviets in the postwar years.[4]

Identifying himself as a senior *partizán* officer, Rudo barked, "Let the kid go, he's one of ours!" The raiders did as they were told—though they continued their "mission" of pillaging the inn, taking whatever cash and bottles of plum brandy they could find before leaving the village.

Rudo reprimanded me for getting mixed up in local matters and ordered me to return to my unit. After the war, I looked him up. He was now Colonel Rudo of the new Czechoslovak Army, and he was the chief examiner of claims for reinstatement of prewar military rank by those who were suspected of collaboration with the Nazis.

Discussing the nature of "*partizán* discipline" somehow always involves executions; this reveals the harsh reality that many of the victims of the Slovak uprising were not necessarily done in by the Nazis. After the failure of the uprising, many of the survivors—often elderly Jews, and women and children—sought refuge in ramshackle woodcutters' huts or in the caves used for storing potatoes. I know of two families from Trenčín who found temporary shelter in such unlikely spaces, only to be robbed and murdered by roving bands of outlaws who were also on the lam.

The Pig and the Peasant

My Russian leaders often sent me into villages seeking food for the team. Sometimes these villages were occupied by German soldiers, and they were always filled with informers itching for a chance to call in the

[4]The weapon Strassmann is describing is undoubtedly the StG 44. Heckler & Koch (which is a German, not Austrian, company founded in 1949) did not develop or manufacture this rifle. The StG 44 or *Sturmgewehr* (from whence we derive the term "assault rifle") was designed and produced by C. G. Haenel Waffen und Fahrradfabrik. Although it is a full-size rifle rather than a machine pistol, it did in fact begin life as the *Machinenpistole 43*, because Hitler demanded more submachine guns and was originally opposed to the idea of a fully automatic or selective-fire main battle rifle; hence the MP 43 nomenclature was a bit of subterfuge. The StG 44 was produced in huge numbers—half a million by war's end—and employed extensively on the Eastern Front. The *Sturmgewehr* did indeed provide the inspiration for the postwar development of the ubiquitous Soviet AK-47.

Ukrainian SS troops (who dramatically responded by thundering in on motorcycles).

On one of these missions, I was dispatched late one night to a cottage at the corner of a small settlement. As a card-carrying *partizán,* I was authorized to ask for a voluntary "gift" of provisions, and if it was not granted, I was empowered to insist upon it—these were hard times for all. Since it was late December, various *partizán* bands must surely have come calling before me. The man of the house knew he would have to give up something, but he pleaded most earnestly that he had hardly enough left to see his family through the winter. He became very agitated, and with all the shouting going on, we disturbed a pig that was hidden behind the stove. When I heard the pig snorting, I became quite annoyed and demanded that he turn the pig over to me. I knew this animal was destined to be the principal source of meat for the family for the rest of the winter. Peasants usually slaughtered a pig around Christmastime and used every part of it as a way of supplementing their protein-poor diet, which was based mostly on potatoes, cheese and bread.

The poor man and his wife started crying, pleading for the life of the pig. They claimed that informers would surely find out that the *partizáns* took the meat, since everybody in this tiny and pitifully poor settlement would know on the following morning that a pig was missing. The peasant pleaded that his family would be killed for feeding the *partizáns.*

By this time, my comrades had arrived. I was commanded to draw my pistol (I had acquired a nice Walther 9mm automatic) and shoot the pig in the head while the rest of the squad was restraining the distraught peasant and his wailing wife. I carried out my orders and we cut the carcass into quarters, leaving a few choice pieces and half of the meat for the family. We then claimed our share and retreated back into the forest. Before we left, the peasant had the good sense to demand a receipt for the confiscated meat, so I scrawled something like: "Pavel Strassmann of the Czechoslovak *Partizáns* hereby certifies that so-and-so gave us a supply of pork in support of the national liberation movement." To complete the documentation in an official manner, I asked how much the pig was worth? Without batting an eye, the peasant replied, "Everything I got." I added, "valued at 50,000 crowns, signed Pavel Strassmann." That was a ridiculously large sum for half a pig, but it didn't matter to me; I just wanted to get out of that settlement without further incident.

In August 1945, I was strolling down a boulevard in Trenčín. I carried that automatic pistol in my hip pocket, because times were uncertain and wartime scores were still being settled. Suddenly I spied this hulking peasant lumbering across the square in my direction waving a rather large stick. I instinctively flipped the safety lever on my pistol and waited to see what he was about. When he got close enough, the big man gave me a bear hug and kissed me! Yes, he was the peasant with the pig. Apparently he submitted the receipt I had given him (along with a pile of other cleverly accumulated papers) and was compensated for his devotion to the cause by being given custody of a farm that had belonged to a Nazi collaborator. The fact that the same farm had originally been expropriated from a Jewish family did not seem to bother anyone.

Hidden History

A definitive historical treatise should be written about the participation of Jews in the Slovak uprising. For example, I have found too many unanswered questions about the organization and fate of the Nováky group.

The Jewish Nováky unit was an organized Allied force, not an irregular collection of armed civilians, as was the case with the Jewish groups that had been operating principally in the forests of Lithuania and Byelorussia. This is an important distinction. So far as I can tell, the Nováky force was the first exclusively Jewish well-organized resistance group engaged in combat since the destruction of a Jewish state by the Romans in 70 C.E. In fact, the Nováky unit preceded by a few weeks the formation of a much better known Jewish unit that became part of the British forces in Libya under the command of General Montgomery.

On the day of the uprising, the arms that had been secretly stored at the Nováky camp in walls and under the kitchen floor were broken out and distributed to selected groups of able-bodied young men. The Hlinka Guard camp guards were disarmed as they fled. The local gendarmes unit also opened its armory to the Jewish inmates. About 200 men ultimately joined this new combat unit.

The Nováky unit immediately proceeded to the nearest army base (at Prievidza) where everyone received Slovak Army uniforms with the new 1st Czechoslovak Army shoulder patch, light arms, and a brief training session which comprised one visit to a local firing range for rifle practice. Three former reserve officers from the prewar Czechoslovak Army assumed command of the new unit, based on their military seniority.

A day later, the Nováky unit received orders from the 1st Czechoslovak Army HQ in Banská Bystrica to proceed to two nearby mining towns with a population consisting mostly of ethnic Germans. The Germans fled without a shot being fired. The Nováky group was ordered to take up fixed positions to prevent an oncoming Wehrmacht unit from occupying a critical rail junction. The untrained defenders prepared hasty fighting positions with the intent of employing conventional defensive tactics. They had rifles, light machine guns, a few heavy machine guns, and one artillery piece, but no communications equipment except for runners. There were no rear echelon support units, no reserves and no artillery to support the Novákys' exposed forward position in an open, flat valley. It was a "do or die" mission.

The vastly more experienced Germans attacked with tanks and other armored vehicles, artillery, mortars and an observation aircraft. In two major assaults, the Nováky unit lost over 20 percent killed and a much larger number wounded before disintegrating as an organized unit. I found out about this battle the following day, when I heard that a number of wounded from Trenčín were housed in a local inn. There I found a cousin, Erich Politzer, and he was in a sorry state—bandaged up and bleeding profusely with no prospects of recovery. Three days later we were forced to abandon the village, leaving the wounded to their fate.

The Surviving Jews

When the Jewish fighters went to war, the rest of the camp population (mostly women, children and those without any combat capabilities) were encouraged to flee back to the communities they had been deported from. Such guidance was offered on the assumption that the Soviet Army would be coming soon to rescue the uprising and secure the hard-won Slovak liberation and freedom. This assumption proved to be terribly wrong. Wherever the Jews leaving the labor camps departed for locations that subsequently became battlegrounds between the *partizáns* and the Germans, only tragedy waited for them. This misfortune was compounded by the migration of Jews into territories that had been liberated by the uprising. Many of these refugees had so far remained hidden from persecution or lived in relative safety under the cover of false identity papers. In the wake of the failed uprising, however, they were rounded up and executed. Many others were deported to concentration camps where the probability of survival was slim at best.

A Military Judgment

In retrospect, I place much of the blame for the unnecessary casualties incurred during the uprising on the leadership; planners who placed untrained volunteers in fixed positions against a well-armed, organized and battle-hardened enemy. This same mistake was repeated time and again during the initial enthusiastic phase of the uprising. To add insult to injury, it soon became apparent that Soviet relief forces would never show up—we were left to fend for ourselves. The regular Czechoslovak Army fared no better: It did not have the means—or the stomach—to make heroic stands.

Partizán casualties during the uprising were also high. We suffered most from having to conduct ambushes on the Germans and the Hlinka Guard without the benefit of any wireless communications, except for links from the Soviet *partizán* battalion HQs to the central *partizán* command in Kiev.

With the onset of winter, disease and freezing became a more lethal enemy than German bullets. Nevertheless, my chances of surviving in a mobile *partizán* band were always better than they would have been had I been a conventional foot soldier facing panzers, mechanized infantry and artillery barrages.

The fundamental tenet of *partizán* warfare is to avoid becoming a target. Conventional units couldn't avoid being constant targets; they gave the Wehrmacht a target-rich shooting gallery, and the Germans took advantage of every opportunity to kill the Slovaks methodically and from a safe distance.

An Assessment

After 1938, the puppet Slovak Republic and its military forces became a committed ally of Nazi Germany. Slovak Army units participated in the Nazi invasion of Poland. They were engaged in major combat against the Soviet Union. Following its alignment with Nazi Germany, the Slovak state formally declared war on the Allies, including Britain and the USA. Consequently, all officers of the Slovak Army were subject to the prevailing rules of war (which the Soviets applied ferociously and cruelly). As I see it, the primary purpose of the Slovak National Uprising was to recast the army as an unwilling participant in the Nazi movement. Being redefined as "freedom fighters" assured that the Slovak military would benefit from the gains of the Allied victors when the war was over. It was hoped that the Slovak leaders and other bad actors would not suffer the penalties of the losers if the Allies recognized the uprising as a legitimate revolt against the Nazis.

When judged from a historical perspective the failed Slovak uprising was a success, especially as seen from the standpoint of the leadership of the Slovak Army; only a very small number of the most outspoken supporters of the Nazi regime were dismissed. If punished at all, they likely only suffered early retirement (with pensions).

MOUNTAINS

Before the collapse of the heart of the uprising in Banská Bystrica, our *partizán* skirmishes took place only on a limited scale. Encounters were precipitated either by raiding parties of the Hlinka Guards or when we engaged in a brief firefight while approaching a target or retreating from the raid. Casualties were very light. Most of the firing was from rifles, punctuated by occasional bursts from a submachine gun. A couple of times we were subjected to a few mortar rounds, but they never landed close enough to cause any casualties.

The weather in western Slovakia was tolerable until the last week in October, then the snow began to fall at the higher elevations where we remained most of the time. Our footprints now left traces of our movements, but it could not be avoided. Compounding this vulnerability was the loss of the leafy cover from the largely deciduous forests. This also limited our ability to make fires, because smoke could be readily seen from miles away by light Fieseler *Storch* observation aircraft, which would radio our position to ground units in the vicinity. Finding a grove of coniferous trees was now a practical necessity; fir trees offered the better cover. They were also a source of branches that could be laid on top of the snow to insulate us from freezing solid to the ground when our body heat melted the snow as we tried to snatch some sleep.

The needles and the pitch-filled twigs found amongst the evergreens were also useful as fire-starters (this was particularly true when the frigid wind was blowing and the all other wood was wet or frozen). To this day, strolling through an evergreen forest over a bed of pine needles gives me more pleasure than viewing even the most fancy rose garden. Where I live now I have three small stands of tall pines with the surrounding ground covered by a thick layer of yellow pine needle mulch. While I was away on a trip, my overly fastidious groundskeeper decided to replace the pine mulch with the more decorative shredded tree bark. Upon my return, I had the expensive tree bark raked out and replaced by the pine needles bedding.

The Base

Immediately after the fall of Banská Bystrica our situation changed radically. Previously we could walk through forests with hardly any interference. Experienced commando raiders well equipped with radios and the benefit of local intelligence from informers now hunted us. I suspect that the Germans also relied on information extracted by torture from captured *partizáns*.

Until the end of October, we remained reasonably safe and camped in remote, well-guarded places. We preferred to stay in villages located at the end of narrow valleys, especially those accessible only through a long, narrow winding road. We posted sentries at points where an approaching vehicle could be detected, giving us sufficient time to escape into the woods. Our favorite villages for overnight stays were Trebichava, Zavada, and Čierna Lehota. Meanwhile, following hard-earned *partizán* experience, we established defensible dugouts on the top of two mountains (Čierny Vrch and Rokoš) to which we could retreat if attacked.

During our raids on the railroads we camped rough with occasional stays in abandoned cottages, barns, or haystacks when we were lucky to find them. With the increase in combat operations in the area in 1944, peasants stopped making hay in the mountain meadows. When the fighting intensified, the peasants and shepherds wisely refused to venture out to the upland pastures. The abandoned stacks of grass generated heat from fermentation, and we found the warmth particularly inviting during the winter. The only disadvantage of bedding down in a haystack was that since they were a favorite of passing *partizáns* and refugees from occupied districts, they were often infested with fleas and lice. Despite that disagreeable aspect, I have a fondness for the smell of rotting grass to this day.

Severe winter weather accompanied by blinding snowstorms arrived in the mountains of Slovakia in the second week of November. We were blissfully unaware that this would prove to be the coldest winter in more than a decade—this in a country where the winters are always harsh. In fact, when I was planning a trip to revisit some of these scenes in mid-May of 1993, I inquired about suitable clothing for my excursions and was warned to bring knee-high boots and a warm coat because it was still snowing on the mountain range that had been the site of some of my adventures.

Retreat to the Mountain

In the second week of November we executed a planned retreat to our prepared base on top of Čierny Vrch mountain. As was our custom, we stayed overnight in one of the outlying villages (Zavada in this case); food and potable water were more accessible in such places. For security, we posted two sentries at intervals on the road leading to the village. The forward sentry would fire at any approaching vehicle and the backup sentry would relay the alarm so we could vanish into the surrounding woods.

This time, however, we miscalculated. The attack force was obviously well trained in dealing with such *partizán* tactics. Instead of coming straight up the road, they detached an element to maneuver around the village and set up an ambush to snare the fleeing *partizáns* after the sentries set off the alarm. We were now without Batko to guide us, but had enough sense to position the squad at the farthest end of the village. When the shooting began, we instantly darted up the hill towards the Čierny Vrch. Although we had to initially pass through an open field to get to the protection of the nearest woods, the shrapnel produced by German mortars missed us altogether. When you heard the distinctive hollow *whoompf* that announced the launching of a mortar round, you hugged the ground and hoped for the best. Once the round had exploded, you could continue running for cover. I believe the mortar fire was employed primarily to pin us down until the German infantry could move in. Also, the shrapnel might catch those who failed to hit the dirt and just kept running out of fear—even an old hand can occasionally lose his nerve.

After the war, I visited Zavada and saw a memorial to those killed that day—mostly villagers, as it so happens. This was of no concern to the

Germans, as such wanton and indiscriminate murder of innocent civilians had the added benefit of serving as a warning to villagers who had the temerity to support the *partizáns.*

When we finally reached our little base on top of the mountain, we were reassured by the clever design of the dugout bunkers; it would take direct hit from a bomb or artillery shell to destroy them. The approaches were narrow defiles that could be easily defended by a small contingent of determined fighters. We hoped it wouldn't come to that.

The base had three of these formidable bunkers, smelly but warm and reasonably dry. The team was divided into several elements, each with a specific task. I was assigned to the foraging group, whose objective was to collect as much food as possible before descent into the snow-laden valley became impracticable.

Strict security measures were put in place; stragglers, as well as men of dubious background, were not allowed to enter the perimeter. In one severe case, a man suspected of being a spy was shot. The rejection of several Jewish families seeking our protection was particularly tragic. Most were former inmates of labor camps in Slovakia and in one instance, we turned away a family that had abandoned a perfectly good hideout to welcome the liberators and the new Czechoslovak territory—this was of course before the collapse of the uprising. Now they were hunted refugees, enemies of the Nazi state. So far as I know all of these families perished.

Rations were distributed twice daily. They generally consisted of bread, smoked bacon, sugar, *slivovic*, and cigarettes. The cook for each dugout also received the meat and other ingredients to prepare a meal. These prepared meals followed an unappetizing routine: boiled pork with cabbage and potatoes, generously dusted with paprika.

It is on the Čierny Vrch where I acquired the habit of claiming my full rations as a *partizán*, which included cigarettes and *slivovic.* As I have already stated, I always traded the cigarettes for bread, and I watched with disgust as men starved themselves to feed their addiction. Initially, I consumed the alcohol ration on the long treks from the mountains. But when I discovered that it made me dizzy and slow-witted, I began to trade it for extra bacon, which provided more calories per pound than any other food source available.

The American

One evening, a Czechoslovak officer came into the dugout and asked for anyone who spoke English. In view of my smattering of English, I volunteered and was immediately assigned to guard a dark-skinned man in civilian clothing, who claimed to be an American airman who had been shot down. He was on his way to Banská Bystrica to be picked up and returned to his base in Italy. This seemed an incredible story to us, though after the war I verified that it was true. Indeed, American B-17s landed in Banská Bystrica twice to deliver weapons and American intelligence officers, and to pick up downed airmen—fifty-six of them! Unfortunately, my American would not be one of them, as by this time the Germans occupied the sole airfield in the liberated sector.

Why he had to be guarded at all was beyond me. I later learned that the Soviets did their best to prevent us from having any contact with the Americans. Since the Slovaks (now the "Czechoslovak Allied Forces") traded American fliers for political and military recognition, the local senior Slovak officer did not wish for any harm to come to my American. Perhaps another reason was a widely circulated rumor that all American fliers had gold coins sewn into their jacket linings to pay off locals who rendered them assistance if they were shot down. While serving in the Pentagon forty-five years later, I found out that this story was true, but that the practice was limited to officers. I had also heard a related tale in which some Russians had purportedly murdered a British journalist who had parachuted into the area to write about *partizán* life. The reporter was killed after a Russian tried to take his jacket. The victim was accused of spying and carrying gold to finance a counterrevolutionary operation.

Many years after the war, I related my story about the airman to a group of air force generals with whom I was having lunch at the Pentagon and they were incredulous; they thought it highly unlikely that the huge Flying Fortresses would be landed on a grass airstrip 350 kilometers behind enemy lines to fetch out American fliers. Then in 1990 I was invited to a fund-raising party for Senator John McCain, who was contemplating a run for the presidency. A spry, elderly gentleman was seated next to me. Of course the topic of war service came up ("Where were you during the war?"), and it turned out that this fellow was a pilot who had been awarded the Flying Cross, and to my surprise, he revealed that he flew one of the downed aircrew pick-up missions to Banská Bystrica! This encounter prompted me to seek out the records of the 483rd Bomb Group (H) and I was able to verify the identity of one George Fernandes, an airman of Portuguese ethnicity—and the man who had been briefly in my custody in 1944. I managed to locate George (he was now an invalid, living at the V.A. hospital in Bellevue, Washington) and gave him a call. We had a pleasant chat, but he remembered little of the episode—only that he had been well fed at a mountaintop partizán base (a tribute to my skills as a forager!).

Subsequently, I delivered several lectures about these American airmen and the disastrous OSS mission in Slovakia in 1944. I now know that the Cold War had already begun by the middle of World War II. I could readily demonstrate that by describing how an American airman had to be guarded by a young Slovak *partizán* to protect him from being spirited away by the Russians.

Gathering Food

We remained sequestered on top of the Čierny Vrch for about a month. During that time, my little group was dispatched on weekly sorties to nearby villages to buy food or, if necessary, take it by force. It took the better part of a day to come down off the mountain over the snow and determine whether it was safe to enter a village. It took another day or more to collect the food and yet another day to scale the steep, icy slopes with our added burden.

Our preferred food source was pigs, but when there were none to be had we settled for sheep. In one instance we also took a goat. The critters were killed, skinned and cut into quarters while we were still in the village. After that, each of us would carry a slab of the meat back up the mountain to the isolated base. We considered these missions to be a privilege, for while we were in the village we stuffed ourselves with food and washed up. But these were also dangerous missions, as we were under continuous threat of a surprise by the Germans or the Hlinka Guards. After a while our visits started forming a pattern, and patterns are never good things in warfare. We should have been more careful.

I remember an incident that resulted from such carelessness. I had just finished checking out a barn where we were to bring a pig for slaughter. Instead of walking on the cow-path behind the houses, I stepped right out into a road intersection. There, staring straight at me from a motorcycle sidecar with a machine gun mounted on it, sat a German soldier in SS uniform. Had I started running, I am sure he would have cut me down with a short burst. Fortunately, I carried my rifle slung upside down and behind me, which must have concealed it somewhat. And it didn't hurt that in my raggedy overcoat and farmer's hat I looked more like a local urchin than a soldier. While the German scrutinized me, I slowly sidled through a nearby garden gate and slunk away, taking great care to close the gate without haste or apparent concern.

After that encounter, I abandoned the idea of collecting any meat that afternoon and made my way to the assembly point for the return to our hideout. The others had received warnings that the Germans were coming; somehow the message never got to me.

Crimes

It is impossible to talk about the *partizán* experience without mentioning the criminality that accompanied such activities. It is a fact that after the uprising all the jails in the liberated districts were thrown open. As a result, there was a large influx of recruits to the Resistance, which criminals found rewarding to join. With an aggressive attitude and talent for stealth, the criminal element proved well-suited to guerilla warfare. Law and order had all but disappeared, and there were unlimited opportunities for robbing and pillaging with impunity. If the victims could be marked as Nazi sympathizers, theft or murder would be justified as a "patriotic" act.

I became involved in a civilian murder (as a bystander) on one of our food-gathering missions to a rural village. As we descended from the mountain and approached the village we saw a large moving van stuck in a ditch. The door of the van was thrown open and a *partizán* band operating in the neighborhood was rummaging through the contents—furniture and all manner of household property. Standing next to the van was a man and a woman who were apparently the owners. The woman was getting very upset and was crying and shrieking in a loud voice that could be heard over quite a distance. Perhaps she said something threatening, I don't know, but when she lurched at the leader of the *partizáns*, he shot her in the head. Her husband jumped to catch the falling woman, and he too was executed. After that, we were invited to help ourselves to the spoils.

One of the men from the *partizán* band that sacked the moving van ended up becoming a member of the Communist Party leadership in Trenčín after the war, even though he had a prewar criminal record. In 1947 I heard rumors that some of the *partizáns* might be prosecuted for crimes committed during the war and I became apprehensive about the possible consequences if I should be called as a witness. In a chance meeting with this same fellow on the Trenčín main square during the Christmas holidays in 1947, he casually suggested that as the son of a prominent capitalist, I would be well advised to get out of the country before the Communists took over. Perhaps he was afraid I would talk and get him in trouble. In any event, this prospect was one of the many reasons I decided to leave my homeland. As it turned out, the Communist takeover occurred in February 1948, ten days after my arrival in England.

Although I did not think so at the time, this thug's warning served me well. I should have seen it as a great favor rather than the threat it was meant to be.

Battle of Magura

The few weeks of staying in the Čierny Vrch dugouts were stressful—brutally cold and demoralizing. But that period was relatively peaceful compared to the nightmare faced by those who had escaped from Banská Bystrica after the uprising collapsed. At least we had a daily routine and nobody was starving. We had adequate supplies to tend to our medical conditions and minor injuries. The news about the failure of the uprising trickled slowly up to us. Only the Soviet team and their radio operator knew the full extent of the debacle, but they weren't talking. We considered ourselves lucky to have avoided the fate of those who were captured. Our leaders tried to cheer us up by assuring us that victory was just around the corner (though no one could tell us when or where the Soviet Army would finally cross the Carpathian Mountains to liberate us). As added relief, our dugouts became less crowded as many of the Slovaks did not return from sorties into the surrounding villages.

Meanwhile, our position was becoming increasingly tenuous as the villages where we customarily obtained supplies were falling under the tightening control of well-organized German patrols summoned by local collaborators as soon as any *partizáns* showed up to collect food.

I believe it was in the second or third week of November that we were roused from sleep in the middle of the night and commanded to prepare for an immediate evacuation of our dugouts; an attack was believed to be imminent. We packed whatever previously accumulated supplies we could carry and set off on a march, not knowing where we were going except that it would be in the direction of the advancing Soviet forces.

We always moved in a single file with enough space between each man so that an ambush would take out as few men as possible. Those walking "point"—at the head of the file where most of the casualties would be sustained—were selected by the senior officer who was usually somewhere near the front as well. The marching order became more important as the depth of the snow increased; the lead man in the file might find himself in hip-deep in snow, and busting trail in deep snow is hard work. Stragglers were left to their own devices; they had to make out as best as they could, and rarely with any help.

We descended the Čierny Vrch in a long line, crossing a valley to ascend an even taller peak, the Magura, where another *partizán* command HQ was located. We made the crossing, which included a roadway, in broad daylight. This made no sense, but I was in no position to question my leaders' decisions. As we marched, other *partizán* groups were falling in with us. It was the first time I had ever seen hundreds of *partizáns* marching as a single group.

After reaching the top of the Magura early in the evening, we continued on a narrow path that ran along the ridgeline of the Mala Fatra mountains. It was still snowing and we had been marching rapidly for twenty hours without a halt. It was now dark and I was somewhere near the middle of the line.

The Ambush

Suddenly bursts from automatic weapons erupted in front of me and I could see the muzzle flashes. We had been ambushed! I could not believe that our attackers would do something like that at night and on top of a mountain. I could just make out a few ghostly figures in white camouflage smocks moving about in the woods, a sure sign we had been set upon by German troops specializing in winter warfare. Acting instinctively, I clutched my rifle and rolled off the trail and down the steep embankment to my right. As I spun downwards I lost much of what I carried in my rucksack, including hand grenades, food and my precious canvas shelter half. I slid down about a hundred feet when a tree finally halted my progress. Crouching behind the trunk I paused to get my bearings and observe what was happening above.

There was wild shooting and shouting everywhere. In a few minutes another body came rolling down the slope. It was Hatlancik, a *partizán* from Trenčín. We were now being approached by what sounded like Ukrainian Vlasov SS troops; they were speaking Russian and pretending to be our comrades. Hatlancik whispered that we should not respond to the calls commanding us to climb back up and resume the march. If I was in any doubt, the occasional reports from small arms convinced me that returning to the top of the ridge was a fool's errand.

Hatlancik and I then moved rapidly down the steep slope of the mountain until we came to the bottom of the ravine where there was a brook. On the opposite side there was an equally steep slope. Now the shooting could be heard coming from all sides except straight ahead. We had no choice; we plunged into the icy water and waded across. I got soaked up to my waist. How we climbed up the opposite slope and continued running away I cannot imagine. Hypothermia was setting in and my teeth were chattering. I had a hard time walking at all or even thinking clearly.

Months later I discovered that only a few of our people managed to escape that well-laid trap. The German plan was a good one; it enabled them to corral and destroy several *partizán* units at once. The tactic involved dislodging small *partizán* bands from multiple hideouts and herding them into a central terrain feature, or "knapsack," where they could be surrounded and eliminated by superior firepower. With the exception of the deep ravine through which Hatlancik and I escaped, all possible routes of egress were cut off by the Germans. We were just lucky.

Shattered Brigades

The survivors of the Mala Fatra ambush reassembled at the few remaining woodland shelters that had not yet been compromised. We could no longer depend on finding quarters within villages, as they were all crawling with Hlinka Guard informers. All that remained were mountainside hay sheds and the like.

The Germans torched any such structure they could find, but there were always enough remaining to offer us a bit of shelter from the elements. How we managed to live under such unsanitary conditions without contracting typhus or some other infectious disease is a miracle. Since we operated in small teams, the opportunities for an epidemic were limited. Anyone who got even modestly sick could not keep up with our marches through the snow and was left behind. Our little band became self-selecting.

Ultimately, we received orders to make our way to an assembly area and then march to camps located to the east, high atop the mountains in central Slovakia. This meant leaving the security of the mountain lairs where we had been licking our wounds and moving into the open and flat Turiec valley—not a very pleasant prospect. From that point, our route of march took us up steep slopes and into the Lower Tatras, about 100 kilometers closer to the area where Soviet and Czechoslovak forces were slowly fighting their way through the Dukla pass leading from the Ukraine.

This road march was a test of endurance. We set out in the second week of December, slogging through hip-deep snow. We crossed two open plains at night to try to avoid a repeat of that devastating ambush. Rather than getting thoroughly soaked in the freezing waters of the Turiec

River, we chanced a bridge crossing. We were very exposed, but managed to complete the operation unmolested.

I cannot adequately describe the effort and the strain involved in this march. We were wet and hungry and suffering from extreme cold and fatigue. Some of the symptoms of hypothermia I had experienced during my escape from the Mala Fatra ambush returned. I became feverish and shuffled along in a daze—I could only focus on the knapsack hypnotically swaying from side to side a few meters ahead of me. Although I was still lugging my rifle, I am not sure I had the strength to load, aim and fire it. As I recall, only about half of the men who started the march arrived at our final destination. Many just gave up and wandered off the path to rest while the somber train of *partizáns* tramped past. Those who fell asleep from exhaustion froze to death. Quite a few managed to hobble to the nearest village and gave themselves up. Such choices were unacceptable to me.

Perhaps my most vivid recollections from this ten-day ordeal are the visions that kept me putting one foot in front of the other without collapsing. To prevent my mind from spiraling into despair, I developed what would become a recurrent dreamlike fantasy that revolved around my idea of the perfect life after the war. My brain kept generating cinematic images, such as walking down the broad boulevards of a great city with skyscrapers, riding in luxurious automobiles to visit lush gardens, or standing in front of a beautiful house with my mother poised in the open doorway reminding me not to be late for Passover dinner. After a few days I could generate such vivid scenes at will. I could even replay my favorites. Once, when my nonsensical babbling became overly agitated, my comrades asked me what was the matter. In my feverish abandon, I explained that I was on my way to America. Subsequently I would tell anyone who would listen that the purpose of the entire march was to get me to America, where I was already expected.

Years later, I learned that such hallucinations are not unusual under conditions of extreme deprivation and fatigue. In many cases, it was just such flights of fancy that kept an individual strong enough to cope with adversity and make it through.

PRAŠIVA

We continued our retreat to higher elevations, moving steadily eastward to reach the area where the central *partizán* command was located. There, we knew we could find shelter—albeit of a rather grim type. There, *partizáns* were holed up in makeshift underground structures following the Russian model, called *zemlyanka*; like a fox, they had literally "gone to ground." These cramped, hastily constructed quarters were little more than continuously leaking ditches whose roofing of ice-covered branches topped with frozen earth kept caving in. They were perpetually filled with the smoke and cloying stench of cooking on improvised stoves. The roofing timbers, which were lashed together with rope and covered with fir branches, sometimes caught fire. These hideouts held two or three tiers of bunks, packing in as many troops as possible. There was a small space near the entrance for storing weapons and only a narrow passageway. The latrines were located some distance away and downhill from the camp, which was both good and bad.

Life in the Zemlyanki

Most of the dugouts that managed to last through the winter were constructed and maintained under the supervision of a *Sibiriak* (Siberian), men with extensive experience in organizing a defensible camp in harsh winter conditions. Clustered among the fir trees, the crude dugouts also offered some protection as bomb shelters, as they were very difficult to spot from the air.

Once snowdrifts blocked the roads that might have allowed German motorized troops to get within reach of our mountain hideouts, we were relatively safe. Many of the surviving *partizán* troops were spared from freezing to death by burrowing into these mountaintop dens. Having moved from shelter to shelter through the end of December, my unit finally settled down in this camp on top of the Prašiva (dusty) Mountain. It was a large complex of more than half a dozen such dugouts, each housing about thirty or forty starving, exhausted and lice-infested *partizáns*.

After the war, I was told that the Prašiva *zemlyanka* compound had been constructed and stocked with provisions weeks before the collapse of the uprising. The camp was originally intended to house the Soviet *partizán* supreme command after the inevitable defeat. I suppose this explains why the Russian command *zemlyanka* (which was guarded by a sentry) always emitted a delicious smell of real food being prepared. We could also hear the Russian officers engaging in rowdy drinking parties late into the night while we were trying to fall asleep with our empty stomachs growling.

There were a few women hanging around the command quarters who had tagged along with the top Soviet officers during the retreat from Banská Bystrica. These exceptionally well-groomed "ladies" (high class camp followers) were of course never seen carrying a weapon. They were rather distinct in that they were attired in the fashionable leather clothing associated with elevated social status in Russia. You could always spot a Soviet commissar by his leather jacket.

The Soviet command post was off limits to us as it also housed a radio transmitter, our umbilical cord to the outside world. There was little contact between the Slovaks and the Russians in any case. I accepted that situation because I respected the Russians' combat, survival, and organizational skills; it was clear that they were far superior to what we were accustomed to from the Slovak Army. They had to be good at survival—after all, they had managed to survive Stalin's regime. These were very tough men. I admired their incredible stamina—whenever we were ready to faint from fatigue, they would break into song; it was their way of dealing with adversity. To this day, I credit the experienced Russian leadership (and a little luck) with my survival.

When we reached the command post on top of the Prašiva, I was fortunate enough to be assigned to a *zemlyanka* for *partizáns* who needed a place to recuperate. Most of us were disabled from exhaustion and frostbite. With the exception of a Russian captain whose leg had to be amputated, I do not recall us carrying any wounded or disabled troopers. Our dugout housed three Jewish doctors. Two of them—Elo Luža and Imre Blau—were young men and quite helpful. The third was an older gynecologist from Bratislava whose name was (I believe) Wertheim; it was his task to inspect and care for the camp followers. The Russians wanted to be sure their kept women were not diseased. This arrangement had many advantages, including the fact that the Russians always gave the doctors extra rations, which they then shared with us. Elo was a practical joker, and it was suspected that he was merely a medical student rather than a full-fledged M.D. He was in charge of rationing scarce medical supplies—a good friend to have.

The most important of these hard-to-get items was the sulfa medication. It proved extremely effective in arresting infection in frostbitten skin, thus preventing the problem from spreading. During the months of constant marching, my feet never managed to get completely dry. My shoes were full of holes and as I had no socks, I wrapped each foot and lower leg with strips of linen. These improvised socks kept slipping when I walked, creating sores; the skin became soft and sloughed off easily. It did not take long before most of the skin below my knees was one large infected sore. Without the daily application of sulfa powder, I do not think I would have ever walked again. I had seen others with gangrenous wounds fall to the wayside and never get back up. I believe there were more *partizán* deaths resulting from freezing while resting than from German bullets.

During the day, repairing the rickety dugouts consumed whatever energy we had. We also had to clear the snow from our stockpile of firewood. When it snowed—which was often—we were charged with clearing a makeshift parade ground, so the commanders could inspect and review us. Such formalities, conducted in gut-penetrating cold, were justified as a way of accounting for everyone as a security measure.

Since the top of the Prašiva was above the timberline and the nearest trees had been cut down to construct the dugouts, our most difficult and time-consuming fatigue duty involved marching down from the mountaintop into one of the steep gullies where fir trees were still standing to obtain firewood. The trees were cut into manageable logs with huge lumberjack-type two-man crosscut saws. Cutting the frozen trees was hard work—it often felt like we were cutting metal, not wood. The logs were then hauled up the hillside with ropes lashed to our shoulders. The most convenient (but surely the wettest) way to accomplish this was to do the dragging on an iced-over creek. Back at camp, the logs were cut into smaller sections, then split into oven-size pieces with axes. The green, frozen wood was poor fuel; it only burned at all because there was sufficient pitch in the pinewood to prime the combustion. It proved adequate to make the limited space in the dugout full of smoke, but pleasantly warm. All of our heat, all cooking and all drinking water (from pots containing melted snow) came from a single cast iron stove.

4. The Prašiva Mountain Range in Winter

Living Conditions

The embers in the stove also proved useful in a unique hygienic application. The Russians in the command dugout had the rare facility for taking a steam bath to cleanse themselves. We did not. Since everyone was full of lice, those of us who could not tolerate hundreds of little insects crawling all over our bodies learned to heat the cleaning rods from our rifles in the fire and apply the searing tip to the seams of our clothing where the lice and their eggs (the nits) clustered. This roasted the little beasties without scorching our underwear too much. Our vermin eradication program became a nightly ritual.

I did not get properly deloused until I was processed into the Czechoslovak Army in the town of Poprad around April 1, 1945. They shaved my entire body and allowed me to shower; after drying off, I was dusted profusely with a medicated white powder that made me quite sick. That was a happy day!

Much of the time in the dugout was spent trying to get some sleep during the long nights in December and January. The only entertainment I recall during this time was the program of dramatic vignettes staged by Elo Luža and an occasional singing performance by a young Russian accompanied by a harmonica. Though I was still suffering from fever, extreme fatigue and perpetual hunger, Elo's colorful sketches stuck in my mind because they always centered on food and women. It appears that prior to the war, Elo made a trip to Paris. His favorite "souvenir" was an especially vivid and detailed memory of each menu offered in the best restaurants. He recalled (or pretended to recall) exactly how the food was prepared and how each dish was served. The entire dugout was in a state of modest starvation, so on particularly trying nights, we asked Elo to recount one of his epicurean delights. These mouth-watering tales always ended with a course of snails served with garlic butter. After such a fine imaginary repast, Elo embarked on an elaborate description of his adventures in some Parisian bordello. I did not understand most of the finer points of his explicit narrative.

Although Elo was once threatened with being shot for his ribald narratives, in truth, we couldn't get enough of them and he was frequently cajoled into giving encore performances. As conditions deteriorated, his most popular story featured a dinner he would be personally serving to the occupants of our dugout immediately after liberation. I think it was not the gastronomic wonders, but the details about the first day after the end of the war that appealed to our imagination.

When the day of liberation finally arrived—May 5, 1945—I really didn't notice anything different about my surroundings. But there was a major change in the way I started thinking about the world. Before VE Day, I could focus on the only thing that mattered—*survival.* After VE Day, everything became possible. And that was quite a burden to place on my sixteen-year-old shoulders.

5. On the Way to the Bratislava Posting, May 1945

Facing Execution (Again)

The worst incident for me during my service as a *partizán* took place in late January 1945. By then I had a fever most of the time and my feet were infected with weeping sores that even the sulfa drugs could not cure. After surviving on a diet of smoked pork fat supplemented by the occasional chunk of pickled uncooked liver, I could no longer keep my food down. Yet I was considered sufficiently able-bodied to pull sentry duty.

At this elevation, above the timberline, the weather was unbearable. A strong, icy wind blew at all times from Poland, with the nighttime temperature occasionally dipping below minus 30 degrees Fahrenheit—it never rose to the freezing point, even during a sunny day.

The sentry schedule called for three-hour shifts. As some consolation, we were issued two shelter halves so we could create a canvas cocoon to keep us from freezing to death. At particularly critical posts, we were provided with a small wooden platform to stand on so our feet wouldn't freeze to the ground. After a week of drawing two daily shifts I was completely exhausted and from a military standpoint entirely useless.

The only relief from this misery was the amazing view from the top of that bald mountain. On a clear and starry night, one could occasionally see flashes of artillery fire in the east signaling the approach of our liberators. It was a glorious sight! I distinctly remember the first time I saw that beautiful fireworks display—it was just after midnight on New Year's Eve, 1945. In my excitement, I alarmed the officer of the guard, who misinterpreted my agitation for concern and told me that the firing was still a great ways off. I must learn how to determine the distance of artillery fire, he said, so I would know when it became a threat. So far as I was concerned, it was not close enough to suit me.

One evening, when I did not return to the bunker at 3 a.m. to wake up my relief sentry, the officer on duty went out to check on me. I have no memory of this, but I was told that I was found huddled on the ground clutching my rifle and shivering. That morning a court martial was convened; sleeping on guard duty was an offense punishable by death. I was not sleeping, I had passed out. I was painfully aware of the fact that an execution pit was only a short distance down the slope from the HQ bunker, and I was equally aware of the nature and swiftness of Soviet military "justice."

Meanwhile, some of the doctors in the compound signed a statement certifying that I had been unfit to perform sentry duty for several weeks and that I blacked out from hypothermia, which technically rendered me a "casualty." The commissar who presided over the proceedings—the soft-spoken Ivanov who knew me from our days with Batko—used this occasion to reprimand the officer in charge of the guards for assigning a useless invalid to such exceptionally harsh and important duty. Still, Ivanov had no choice but to observe the regulations, and the mildest sentence available for my "infraction" was plenty severe: I had to leave the camp.

To my way of thinking, banishing me from the encampment to a place where I could recuperate was little more than a deferred execution. If I didn't die from exposure (which was highly likely), I would certainly be easy prey for such wolves as German patrols or banditti. I was ordered to embark on a long trek through deep snow to what was believed to be the relatively safe mountain village of Liptovska Lužna. There I was to seek out a particular innkeeper (a friend to the *partizáns*) who would perhaps care for me. I was later informed that Ivanov had taken pity on me because he knew I was a good soldier; he had even recommended me for a decoration of some sort, but it had fallen through the cracks.

My three weeks in Liptovska Lužna were spent almost entirely in sleeping. Upon my arrival in this village, a poor woodcutter named Valent Serafin saw my weakened condition and took me in. During the first few days, as I was teetering on total collapse, Valent and his wife nursed me and fed me mashed potatoes as well as a local variety of cottage cheese—soft food was all I could handle. After that, I was shuttled from house to house, usually ending up in hutches or outbuildings where the peasants kept their livestock. I particularly remember a very kind gentleman by name of Knobloch; he was an American of Slovak descent who came to this strictly Catholic village as a Baptist missionary before the war. He arranged for me to stay with a Baptist family of weavers for a few days. I hallucinated much of the time, but at least my persistent fever began to subside and the festering sores on my feet started the slow healing process.

When I was leaving Czechoslovakia in February of 1948, I could not take any Czechoslovak currency with me. From the post office in Prague I mailed Valent a postal check for all the money I had left after receiving my share from the sale of some of my father's properties. In those days, that would have been a huge sum. When communications with Communist Czechoslovakia finally resumed forty years later, I tried to contact Valent. I was told that he took a job building timber scaffolding in the uranium mines in the early 1950s. He did not live long after that. Nobody in the uranium mines did.

LIBERATION

The military situation in Slovakia in the spring of 1945 was very muddled. War was being waged in valleys and similar outposts that could be easily defended by relatively few German troops who were determined to fight to the death. The defenders were dug in to prepared positions from where they could inflict heavy casualties, which in turn meant that the Soviet advance through the Slovak mountain passes was much slower than we expected. Here and there the Russians employed the *partizáns* to harass the Germans' rear areas and supply lines, but that made little difference. The main thrust of the Russian offensive was directed across the Hungarian plains, where Soviet armored columns could make good progress.

Following the incident in which I came to the defense of the innkeeper in Liptovska Lužna, I was ordered to leave the village by Lieutenant Rudo. I was in no shape to make the long hike back up the Prašiva mountain and as the nearest *partizán* encampment was only a few kilometers away in the settlement of Železno, that is where I decided to go. When I showed up, I discovered that it was under the command of a regular Czechoslovak Army major who had the unbelievable name of Vražda ("murder" in Slovakian). The *partizán* detachment was made up of former Slovak gendarmes and a few ex-army officers who managed to escape deportations to German labor camps. They were pretty much all sick and unfit for combat. The village had been a spa and sanatorium in better times, and while the rooms in the sanatorium had beds, furniture, and even running water, there was no heat. We therefore burned the furniture to keep warm. In my view, the entire setting looked better than a royal palace!

To my great and pleasant surprise, here in Železno I ran into Luža and Blau, the two doctors I knew from the Prašiva cantonment. They had brought a number of sick *partizáns* here for rest and medical treatment, and as I recall, five American fliers. The Americans kept to themselves. Meeting up with the doctors was timely for me, because I had started coughing up profuse amounts of blood, a symptom that Blau diagnosed as an advanced stage of pleurisy. That was not good news for me.

In the first week of March, we received orders to ready ourselves for a move toward the front, which was now close enough so that at night we could distinguish individual rounds from the approaching cannonade. Staying in Železno was also becoming dangerous, as it could become a battleground at any moment. The problem was that nobody knew exactly how far we would have to walk to cross the front lines and reach the safety of the liberated zone.

I think that it must have been some time around the middle of the month when I finally set out on my last march to the east—and I once again found myself scaling steep mountains still covered with deep snow.

Vražda wisely chose to follow a difficult trail that bypassed the valleys where Russian and Rumanian soldiers were advancing slowly and methodically against the German rearguard troops. Most of the time, we picked our way along logging trails high up along the slopes of the mountainside. Clearly, others had used this trail; there were signs of desolation everywhere. We encountered many decomposing corpses as well as dis-

6. Paul's Passport Picture, 1947

carded items of clothing. We reasoned that these paths must have been used by retreating *partizáns*. The bodies looked like they had been there since the fall. By steering clear of the valleys, we hoped to avoid being attacked by trigger-happy Germans as we marched east and again by the Russians, who might very well mistake us for Germans (as we would be approaching from the west). It was a sticky situation.

On the morning of March 20, 1945, without a shot being fired and without much of a fuss, our sorry-looking column hobbled across the lines into what was now liberated country. Lethargic Rumanian sentries paid us little heed. They waved us on and directed us to proceed down a paved highway to the Soviet military checkpoint.

It was then that I realized that for me, the war was over.

TRANSITION

The minute I set foot in the liberated sector of Czechoslovakia, I was free of the oppression that began in 1938.

Walking down a road for the first time in seven months without fear of being shot at was a feeling I could not easily get used to. Freedom did not present itself as a sudden wonderful relief from all troubles, as I had imagined. It dawned on me that I did not have the slightest idea what to do next except to get my infected and painful molars pulled in a barbershop that happened to be open in the next village.[5]

It took a few days for our group to be processed by what was obviously an NKVD operation. The Americans did not have to wait. A Czechoslovak Army staff car picked them up and ferried them to headquarters. *Partizáns* with proper identification as well as Slovak soldiers still in uniform had to march for another day to a place where buses picked us up for delivery to the recruiting offices of the Czechoslovak Army in the town of Poprad.

The army medic who examined me did not spend more than a few minutes before stamping me as unfit for military service on account of "advanced pleurisy." I was in sufficiently bad shape that I was immediately carted to a formerly posh hotel in Tatranska Lomnica, which was converted into a hospital, now filled with wounded and sick soldiers and *partizáns*. It was heaven to be sleeping in beds with clean sheets and access to an unlimited supply of bread, jam, sugar and running hot water.

---

[5]From the Middle Ages through the mid-eighteenth century, the barber-surgeon was a skilled tradesman whose practice was ancillary to the physician's profession. Barbers continued to perform basic dentistry in rural villages (where doctors were few and far between) as a matter of necessity, and in some underdeveloped areas they still do.

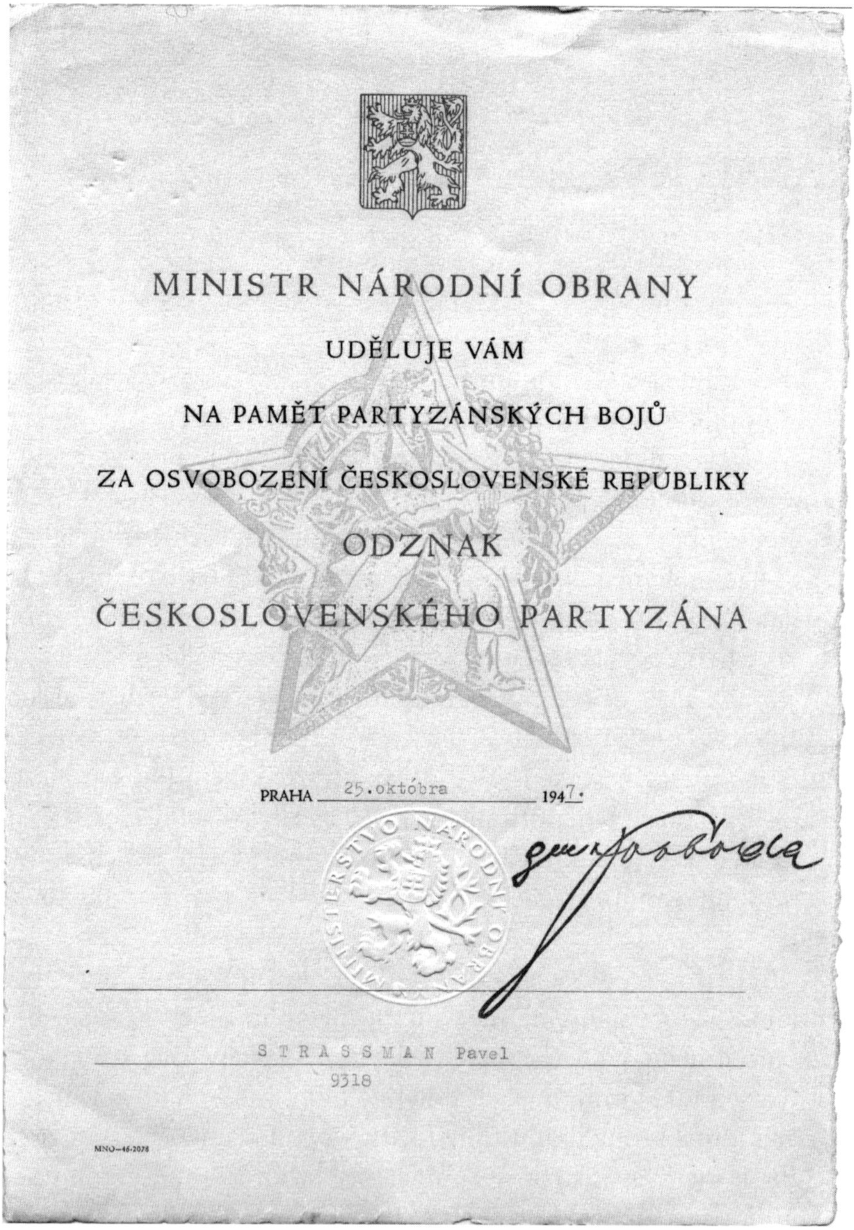

MINISTR NÁRODNÍ OBRANY

UDĚLUJE VÁM

NA PAMĚT PARTYZÁNSKÝCH BOJŮ

ZA OSVOBOZENÍ ČESKOSLOVENSKÉ REPUBLIKY

ODZNAK

ČESKOSLOVENSKÉHO PARTYZÁNA

PRAHA 25.októbra 1947.

STRASSMAN Pavel

9318

MNO–46-2078

7. Grant for *Partizán* Badge

The hotel had recently been abandoned by Nazi officers and the basement was full of small arms ammunition as well as a cache of still-crated shoulder-fired antitank weapons that the Germans called *panzerfaust*. Along with several other young firebrands, I was enlisted by the hotel custodian to dispose of these lethal rockets by firing them into a concrete shed flanking the hotel tennis court. What fun!

As soon as I was sufficiently mobile, I also amused myself by writing several short stories that advocated *partizán*-type vengeance against

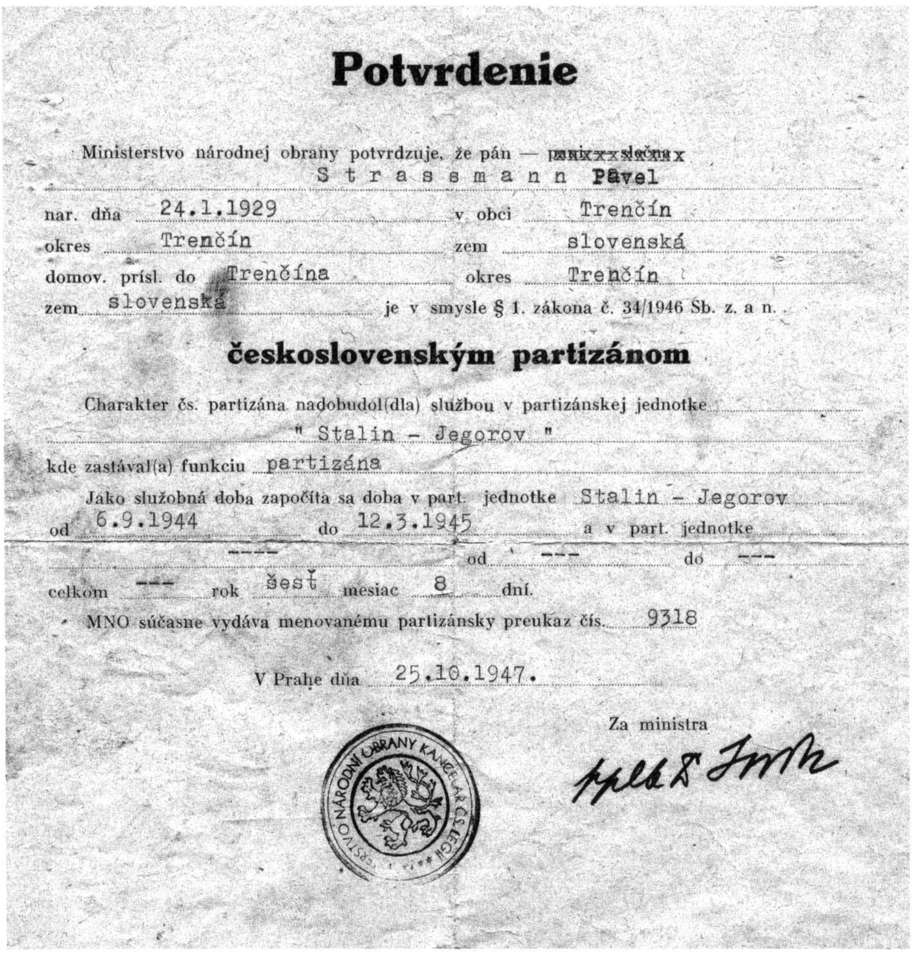

Potvrdenie

Ministerstvo národnej obrany potvrdzuje, že pán — S t r a s s m a n n Pavel

nar. dňa 24.1.1929 v obci Trenčín

okres Trenčín zem slovenská

domov. prísl. do Trenčína okres Trenčín

zem slovenská je v smysle § 1. zákona č. 34/1946 Sb. z. a n.

československým partizánom

Charakter čs. partizána nadobudol(dla) službou v partizánskej jednotke " Stalin - Jegorov "

kde zastával(a) funkciu partizána

Jako služobná doba započíta sa doba v part. jednotke Stalin - Jegorov od 6.9.1944 do 12.3.1945 a v part. jednotke ---- od --- do ---

celkom --- rok šesť mesiac 8 dní.

MNO súčasne vydáva menovanému partizánsky preukaz čís. 9318

V Prahe dňa 25.10.1947.

Za ministra

8. Certification as Czechoslovak *Partizán*

Nazis and collaborators. These articles were pinned up on a news items wall display which became the principal source of war news in the absence of other media. Captain Nicholas Langer, the local commissar, complimented me on my bloodthirsty style.

After about two weeks of this bliss, recruiters showed up at the hospital seeking to recruit "politically reliable" ex-*partizáns* for an officer course that was starting up in two days. Although at the time it was not clear to me what this was all about, Langer volunteered me, as he thought I was a suitable prospect who was itching to get back into action before the war came to an end.

The objective of that school was to send former *partizáns* to join the military police and conduct purges of undesirables in the newly occupied territories. Because I spoke some German I expected to be assigned to the Sudetenland, the region that was populated by ethnic Germans who were Hitler's pretext for dismembering Czechoslovakia in 1938. There were scores to be settled and I was certainly thought to be the type who would do whatever needed to be done, to include a sort of reverse ethnic cleansing. The group of officer candidates was a motley crew, indeed; it included my bunkmate, Jozef Staudinger, who subsequently became one of the judges who sentenced Father Jozef Tiso to hang.

I never made it to the Sudetenland. The war ended on May 5, and when our advance troops arrived in the borderland, all of the Germans had (wisely) gone away.

At graduation in the second week of May 1945, I was the only member of the class who was not rewarded with a commission, because the head of the school found out that I was only sixteen. All I got was the enlisted rank of a full corporal in the Czechoslovak Army, as well marching orders to leave for Bratislava as a bodyguard to a colonel in the military police.

Smartly turned out in my new uniform with an automatic pistol on my belt, I stopped by my old house in Trenčín. So far as I knew, my mother would still be hiding somewhere (if she was alive) and my sister might still be wandering through the countryside with forged identity papers. When I queried the neighbors, there was no news about anybody. I did manage to discover that my mother and sister had been captured and packed off to internment camps Germany. My father and grandparents had also been deported. I was alone.

I tarried in Trenčín for only one day and enjoyed how some of my former hecklers now cowered when they saw me in my new uniform. I strutted around the main square for a while, but I had no desire to settle old scores. Despite fantasies about retribution that I had been nursing for months, I peacefully departed to Bratislava to report to my new army post.

I only stayed in the army for another three months. I didn't like it because most of my work involved expediting mountains of paperwork and running errands because electronic communications were unreliable. There were no purges to conduct; a Byzantine bureaucracy was installed that let just about all of the perpetrators off the hook. Nor was ethnic cleansing necessary, since all Germans and their collaborators had fled to the American-occupied zone in western Germany.

My boss in Bratislava was now-Colonel Nicholas Langer. After appraising the situation he ordered me to get out of the army because there was no career there for a sixteen-year-old Jewish boy without any education.

In the fall of 1945, my sister made her way back from a slave labor camp and I roomed with her in Trenčín for a while. None of the rest of the family every resurfaced. The time had finally arrived to resume a normal life, to start organizing for a new existence and to start forgetting about the lost years. My first priority was to obtain a passport to leave the country. It took a great deal of effort, unending paperwork, divestment of all claims on property, a certificate of political reliability and a hefty bribe to finally obtain a passport which would enable me to get out of Czechoslovakia. It took me until October of 1947 to accomplish that.

In due course I received the official documents authenticating my participation in the uprising and subsequent *partizán* operations. This certification became the basis for receiving back pay from the Czechoslovak Army for the entire period served.

Sachsenhausen

Sometime in June we received our father's only, his last, communication since he was seized by the Gestapo eight months before. The letter,

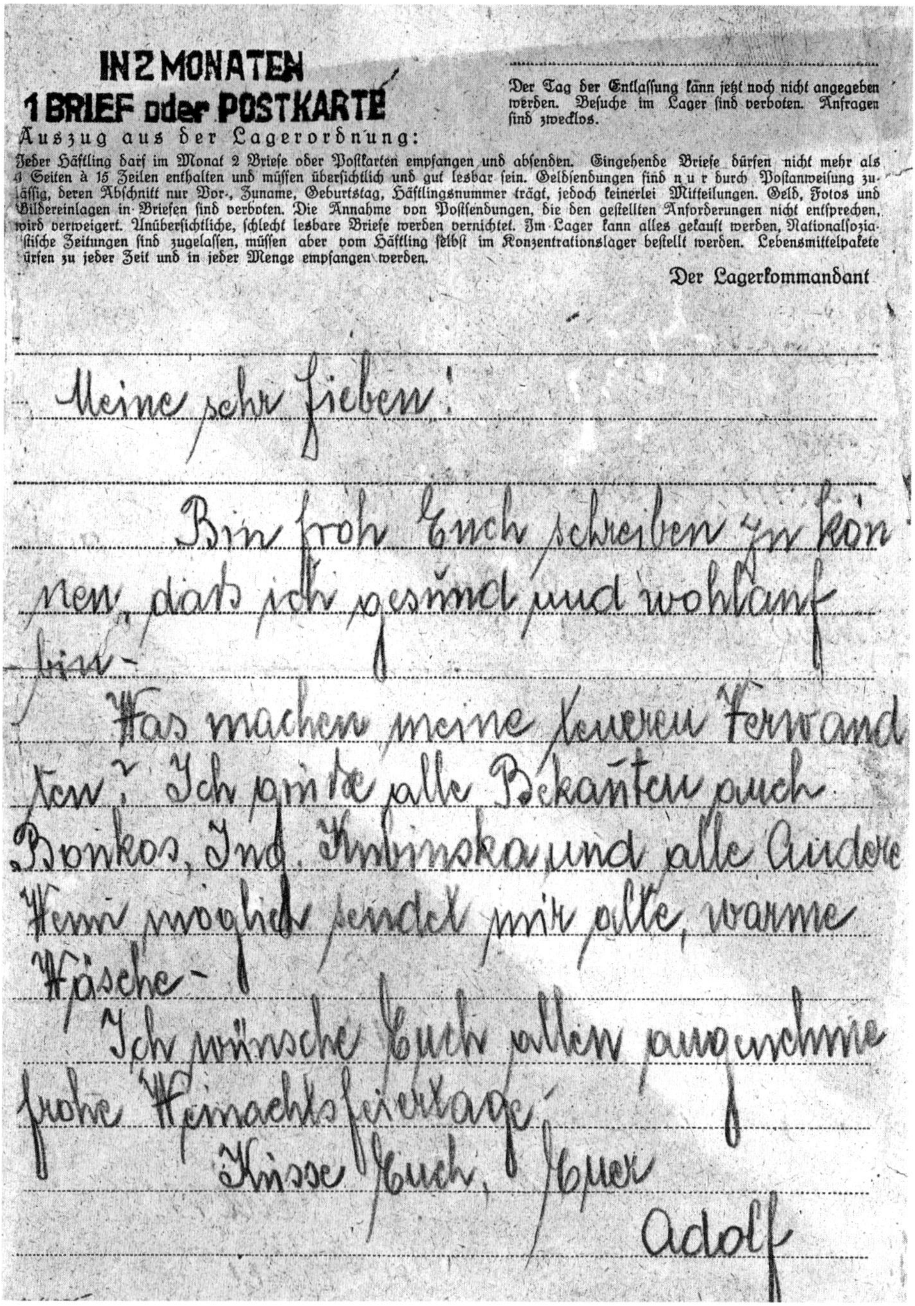

IN 2 MONATEN
1 BRIEF oder POSTKARTE

Der Tag der Entlassung kann jetzt noch nicht angegeben werden. Besuche im Lager sind verboten. Anfragen sind zwecklos.

Auszug aus der Lagerordnung:

Jeder Häftling darf im Monat 2 Briefe oder Postkarten empfangen und absenden. Eingehende Briefe dürfen nicht mehr als 4 Seiten à 15 Zeilen enthalten und müssen übersichtlich und gut lesbar sein. Geldsendungen sind nur durch Postanweisung zulässig, deren Abschnitt nur Vor-, Zuname, Geburtstag, Häftlingsnummer trägt, jedoch keinerlei Mitteilungen. Geld, Fotos und Bildereinlagen in Briefen sind verboten. Die Annahme von Postsendungen, die den gestellten Anforderungen nicht entsprechen, wird verweigert. Unübersichtliche, schlecht lesbare Briefe werden vernichtet. Im Lager kann alles gekauft werden, Nationalsozialistische Zeitungen sind zugelassen, müssen aber vom Häftling selbst im Konzentrationslager bestellt werden. Lebensmittelpakete dürfen zu jeder Zeit und in jeder Menge empfangen werden.

Der Lagerkommandant

Meine sehr Lieben!

Bin froh Euch schreiben zu kön-
nen, daß ich gesund und wohlauf
bin.
Was machen meine teueren Verwand-
ten? Ich grüße alle Bekanten auch
Bonkos, Ing. Kubinska und alle Andere.
Wenn möglich sendet mir alte, warme
Wäsche.
Ich wünsche Euch allen angenehme
frohe Weinachtsfeiertage.
Küsse Euch, Euer
Adolf

9. Father's Letter from Sachsenhausen

which was posted April 7, 1945, came from Oranienburg, Germany (near Berlin). He was identified as Israel Adolf Strassmann, #42690, Block 15, Sachsenhausen Camp. The letter was addressed to our neighbor, Mr. Kišš, a close family friend who had served as our godfather when the family was baptized in 1942.

In his letter, Father is inquiring about a place called Kubinska, where my mother had gone into hiding.

Judging from his firm handwriting, he must have still been in reasonably good health. The Sachsenhausen camp was liberated two weeks later. But on the eve of the inevitable liberation, 33,000 prisoners were forced out of the camp to begin a Death March. They were divided into groups of 400. The Nazis planned to corral them on ships, put them out to sea and then sink the ships. They were inhuman! Thousands of the inmates died during the course of the march, as they were without food, water or shelter. The SS shot anyone who became too weak to continue. When they liberated Sachsenhausen, Soviet soldiers found only 3,000 survivors in the camp, most of whom were starving, ill and too weak to even welcome their liberators. Despite the medical attention they received, most of the survivors succumbed in the days to follow.

There was really nothing left to keep me any more in Slovakia. I had to leave to start a new life somewhere where I would not be haunted by the people and places that kept reminding me of the experiences of the war years. If I could make it to America somehow, I could perhaps close a chapter of my life that I still can't help calling "my war."

Part II

The Way We Were

ORIGINS

I was born in Trenčín, Czechoslovakia and much of my story revolves around my life and experiences in and around that town until I left it forever ten days before the Communist takeover in 1948.

Trenčín is one of the oldest Slovak cities. Strategically sited on the river Váh near three passes through the Carpathian Mountains, it was bound to become a center of trade and commerce as well as a key point of military interest. Early settlement dates back to the Bronze Age, and having driven the Celts and the Germanic tribes out of the region, the Romans established an outpost there in the second century C.E. The legionnaires left an inscription on what is now the castle rock touting a victory over the Germans in the year 179. This bold proclamation sparked my youthful imagination and led to my lifelong interest in history.

Beginning in the era of the Great Moravian Empire, Trenčín served as a cultural, administrative, and military center for the region; it is possible that the oldest stonemasonry of the castle—the rotunda—was constructed during this period. Having been briefly claimed by Poland, Trenčín was absorbed into the Kingdom of Hungary early in the eleventh century, and there it remained until the close of World War I. It is notable that during the Mongol invasion of 1241, Trenčín castle was one of the few strongholds in Eastern Europe that successfully repelled the marauding armies of the Golden Horde.

Medieval Trenčín was designated a free royal town by King Zigmund in 1412. This act resulted in the chartering of the craft guilds that made the town a center of commerce for merchants and craftsmen, a status it enjoyed for many years to come. In 1890, with a population of 5,100, Trenčín boasted 174 shoemakers and 106 tailors.

10. The Trenčin Castle (1998). B = Paul's Birthplace

Shifting Fortunes

Over the centuries, poor Trenčín found itself thrust into the crucible of history. Its saga is one of wars, floods, fires, plagues, political intrigue, and occupation by a succession of oppressive rulers. In 1790, a devastating conflagration gutted the once-proud castle, and it remained untouched for over 150 years. The picturesque ruin passed through the hands of various private owners during the late nineteenth and early twentieth centuries and generally suffered from neglect. Finally, the entire decaying pile was donated to the city in 1953 and proclaimed a National Cultural Monument. It has since undergone extensive restoration, rising phoenix-like from its ashes to become a popular tourist attraction.

The constantly shifting political landscape had a profound effect on the peasantry and townsfolk. In each case, some profited while others suffered. Fortunes could be lost overnight through physical destruction or expropriation when new rulers assumed power. There was a sense of ebb and flow over the centuries: When the newly formed Czechoslovak government took over in 1919, the peasantry benefitted from what was labeled as "land reform"; then when the Slovak Republic was established in 1939 (through the "beneficence" of the Nazis), much of this property was redistributed to the Hlinka Slovak People's Party faithful; this handoff was repeated in 1942 when the assets of Jews were seized, and again in 1945 with the confiscation of property illegally acquired by Nazi collaborators. When the Communists came to power after the war, all property was nationalized. The most recent redistribution took place in 1998 in the wake of the collapse of the Soviet Union. Life goes on.

Echoes of the Past

My childhood was shaped by encounters with ghosts. On the street leading to the castle, there was a house that had served as the living quarters of the local executioner until the beginning of the nineteenth century. On my way to the river, I passed brooding ramparts where "witches" were burned. As evidence of the town's violent past, one could see cannonballs embedded in the walls around the massive town gates. My elementary school was constructed in such a way that one of the corridors included a section of the fortress wall. The castle keep served as our favorite playground; we clambered through abandoned dungeons and routinely rooted up crusty artifacts of indeterminate vintage. I was steeped in history and it made an indelible mark on my consciousness.

The Industrial Revolution brought French textile firms to Trenčín seeking cheap labor, and by the second half of nineteenth century the town had developed into a vibrant manufacturing hub. The presence of many industrial enterprises and financial institutions buttressed by a railway connection to Žilina, across the Carpathian Mountains on the way to Poland, contributed to an economic boom based around the manufacture of clothing and foodstuffs.

Although the worldview of most Jewish youths in Eastern Europe was formed in agricultural surroundings and dominated by staunch religious teachings, my own upbringing reflected exposure to industrial, military, secular, and commercial culture.

The center of Trenčín—the "old town"—was situated within the formidable walled enclave separating the town from the fortifications of the castle. My grandfather's house was one of the prominent homes facing the square. Radiating out from the walled main square were streets that reflected the growth of the town. My father opened his business in the most desirable district for retail establishments in 1919, relocating to a new building in 1934 as he continued to prosper.

Trenčín was a prized possession for any medieval regime. Its commercial trade, guilds and services generated healthy tax revenues for the rulers and provided a reasonable quality of life for the citizens, who enjoyed generous municipal liberties. In due course, such traditions were extended to Jewish traders and professionals, making the town an attractive location in which to settle and raise a family.

The military presence was a prominent feature of the town—and an attraction for a young boy. Because of its location, Trenčín played host to an army garrison since time began. During my youth, a large military complex was located at each end of the town. In the surrounding fields there were remnants of ammunition dumps. Across the river was a mock battlefield, with trenches, bunkers, and machine gun emplacements that were used in training exercises. One could not avoid observing the daily company drills on the large pasture only a few hundred yards from the center of town. My fascination with the maneuvers of the locally-quartered 71st Infantry Regiment of the Austro-Hungarian Army often made me late for my piano lessons. I also had a personal connection with the regiment, as the father of one of my close friends was a major in the 71st.

The sense of history, the pervasive institutional violence and regime change, the constant military presence—all became formative influences, molding my young mind in more ways than I knew. In many ways, they prepared me for the approaching hardships.

FAMILY

January 24, 1929, (the date of my birth) was one of the coldest days in Trenčín in over a century—and that in a country where the winters were always very severe.

11. Birthplace, Grandfather Strassmann's House

This ancient town that had for so long been a part of Hungary (later Austro-Hungary) subsequently split into the Czechoslovak Republic, then separated again to form the Slovak state. After the Second World War, it was reconstituted as part of Czecho-Slovakia, and is now the Slovak Republic. All of those changes occurred in less than a century. My political sensibilities were sharpened by the fact that in my youth I had the experience of living under three different political regimes and had been subjected to the occupation of three different armies.

Father

Adolf Strassmann was born in 1894 in Horny Lideč, a small Moravian village not far from Trenčín. He was murdered in Germany at the age of fifty-one in April 1945.

Father was a physically vigorous, stern, independent-minded, and decisive former military man. My mother and his friends called him "Adko," but in affectionate moments Mother called him "Joni." Father graduated from a commerce academy in Vienna, which was an exceptionally high level of achievement in those days. One of his many admirable traits was his penmanship. All of his ledger entries were neat, precise and highly organized. In those days, penmanship and clarity in record keeping were among the primary requirements for holding a trusted position in a company.

Thanks to his education and readily apparent leadership qualities, he received a commission in the local regiment of the Austro-Hungarian Army at the beginning of the First World War and served with distinction in Russia, Bosnia, and Italy.

12. Father on his Favorite Black Horse, Zigany, in Bosnia

By the time of his discharge, he had been promoted to the rank of major in a combat command—most unusual for a Jewish man in those times. During the campaign in Italy he was wounded by an artillery shell that landed nearby. Not all of the metal was removed at the time, and I recall that it was not until 1936 that a remaining fragment worked itself far enough out of his calf to be surgically extracted. His many medals (along with that last bit of shrapnel) were kept in a box in a drawer in my parents' bedroom, right next to my mother's favorite cologne, No. 4711.

After Father returned from the war, he established a modest grocery store. Subsequently he expanded it into a flourishing wholesale food and agricultural products distribution firm. He grew the business rapidly during the 1930s despite the economic blight that was smothering Europe. Father became one of the dominant merchants in the Trenčín district, with two diesel trucks delivering merchandise to retail stores throughout the surrounding villages.

13. Father in the Early 1920s

I vividly remember the daily routine: Our chores began before six o'clock in the morning, summer and winter, with the filling of orders and staging the items in the yard for pickup by a crew of workmen. These fellows loaded the goods onto trucks or horse-drawn wagons for delivery.

I can still smell the aroma of roasting coffee; we roasted a fresh twenty-kilo batch of coffee beans on a hand-turned wood-burning roaster every other day. At least once a week, the manually-powered machine was used for roasting peanuts, or "American nuts," as we called them. It often fell to my lot to crank the handle of the roasting drum, inserting a sampler through the axle every so often to see if the coffee was of the right dark brown color. When the beans were done they were dumped onto a large copper screen and quenched with a bucket of water.

My parents worked with intense diligence. After they supervised loading the wagons and trucks, the doors were opened to the retail trade. The store closed down at noontime for a lunch break and re-opened at three o'clock in the afternoon, often staying open until as late as nine o'clock at night. Those were the store hours six days a week; we were also open for a half-day on Sundays, when the peasants from the neighboring towns came to hawk their produce on the marketplace and then do their shopping in the local stores. In a traditional arrangement that carried over from pre-industrial times, my family lived in an apartment above the store.

Father's War

My father went into the First World War as the commanding officer of the local infantry company. During the war years, he forged close ties with his men, many of whom had been drafted from the surrounding villages and countryside. Father was enormously respected because he always tried to prevent the needless loss of life produced by senseless bayonet charges against machine guns—a favorite tactic of the Austrian generals (who didn't have to take part in such wholesale slaughter).

Father's commercial success owed much to his deep regard for his fellow veterans, many of whom had become shopkeepers in the neighboring villages; he always knew who could be trusted for an extension of credit. That was the principal reason why many local distributors of agricultural products were switching their business to our wholesale firm.

I do not think that the modern military has a full appreciation of the way the army was organized in the Austro-Hungarian Empire. In a semi-feudal throwback, conscripts were almost entirely drawn from local villages and the companies were named after their towns; regiments bore the commander's name. In those days, the commanding officer had enormous power and virtual autonomy, receiving from the army only uniforms, weapons, ammunition, and cash to meet the payroll. Food, medical care, and transport were usually obtained from local villages, especially as the war progressed and military logistics became increasingly unreliable. As a result, the well-being of a unit depended largely on the quality, energy, and it should be said, ingenuity of its leadership.

Mother

My mother, Frances, or Františka (her friends called her "Franzi"), was born in Budapest in 1904. She was an independent and strong-willed lady, but very even-tempered. She came from a family of craftsmen rather than traders (as was more often the case with the Jews). Father married her in 1924; the wedding was at the Scheibner Hotel, then the only kosher hotel in town. I was the second child, preceded by my sister Ella, who was born in 1925. Franzi had a reputation as a practical, honest, and caring friend.

My mother was a beautiful, hardworking woman. She was a full partner with my father in business affairs, sharing the heavy burdens of building a business while also managing our household. She functioned as the cashier in the store and the peacemaker in both the store and our extended family—our business had a dozen employees who did not always get along.

14. Parents' Wedding Picture, 1924

My sister, who shared those last days with my mother in the camp at Ravensbruck, said that Mother's only regret about her life was that she had not spent as much time with her children as she had wished. My mother used to call me "*spaček*," the Slovak diminutive for the little starling bird that was known to be daring, curious, and a nuisance. This was certainly a good characterization of my childhood behavior. I shared my parents' independent spirit and was frequently punished for all sorts of trespasses, including an inclination to experiment with forbidden things and organizing elaborate pranks.

15. Mother as a Young Girl

In 1940, my mother had to leave her position in the business. She was summarily dismissed from her job as the cashier in the Strassmann store. The entire enterprise was taken over by a government-appointed *arizator* (a member of the fascist party who was assigned as an agent to convert the Strassmann business into an Aryan enterprise). My father remained in the store as the lowest-paid employee. He was the only one who was qualified to continue running the operations of a business that provided food supplies for the entire Trenčín district.

My mother then tended to the household exclusively, assuming the duties of the nursemaid and the cook; those domestics had to be dismissed when our family was squeezed into only two rooms. Ironically, I got to see the most of my mother when these troubled times had arrived, this despite the everyday distractions—including the incessant hunt for food—that claimed her attention. In those lean days, it was remarkable how our household always had plenty to eat, including fresh fruit and vegetables.

Mother's gentile friends always made sure she received an adequate supply of the current crop. With limited refrigeration capacity, most of the fruit was stored on top of the dresser in my parents' bedroom. We were only allowed to eat the fruit when brown spots began to appear on the skin. Nevertheless, she always managed to assemble food packages, including canned goods and smoked sausages, to send to the less fortunate in the concentration camps. It was my job to make up the parcels and deliver them to the post office.

Family Life

Of the photos I have of my family, many were taken in the 1930s while we were on vacation in the Tatra Mountains. My parents were avid hikers and this was my father's favorite spot. The last few family pictures I have were taken on the terrace of our home—just prior to our eviction. As conditions worsened, the terrace offered the only sanctuary where we could gather for a few moments of peace.

16. Parent's Last Picture Together, 1941

My earliest childhood memories are of the family rituals that revolved around Jewish holidays. The peak holiday was of course Passover; it triggered a flurry of activity that was supervised by my mother. All the dishes and utensils had to be exchanged for a more formal kosher set that were kept in the attic, and all sorts of tasks were undertaken to conform to the prescribed rituals (among which was the preparation of a carp in aspic and a roast goose). I always ran errands for my mother to help out. By the age of seven, I had learned how to pull dough to make the thin strudel pastry, and to knead flour, yeast, sugar, and butter together to produce dumplings.

My father gave the appearance that he was modestly religious, but I always suspected that he was really an agnostic. Mother insisted on keeping a kosher household though, largely out of respect for my devout grandfather, Alexander, who lived with us. In our kitchen, we separated the *fleishig* (meat) dishes and utensils for serving meals from the *milchig* (dairy) dishes and those for meals that would be touching any milk products. Adherence to a kosher kitchen was a great burden and we therefore employed additional help before and during the holidays. All of the dishes had to be carefully washed in separate batches to conform to our religious doctrine. Just consider the burdens this imposed on my mother: Our kitchen was equipped with a wood-burning stove and only cold running water. For dishwashing, we had to heat water in a huge pot. The pot had to be struck briskly with a hammer to chip off the steadily accumulating layers of calcium deposits formed from the city water supply.

Running the household was incredibly labor intensive. I still do not understand how my mother managed the cooking and washing while taking care of the business and family affairs. I remember that the job of washing my sister's hair was always a major affair, because Mother insisted on using only calcium-free water and soap that did not leave any residue on my sister's raven locks—we kept a rain barrel especially for the purpose.

Even though we were considered to be one of the most prosperous Jewish families in town and lived in a modern dwelling built in 1934, we still depended on cold running water throughout the house. The most "modern" feature of our home was the steam heating for the central living area. It worked just fine, though it occasionally emitted strange burbling noises when the steam condensed faster than the heat that came up from the basement, three levels below. We burned anthracite coal to heat the remainder of the house; it was delivered once a year and required an elaborate fire-starting routine that was a real nuisance on a cold morning. Only the main bathroom had hot running water and even then only when the wood-burning copper stove in the bathroom was lit. I had to carry wood up from the basement every Friday ("bath day") to feed the beast. We also had a wood-burning stove in the attic for heating water for the weekly washing of linens. That of course added an additional flight of stairs to my wood delivery chores.

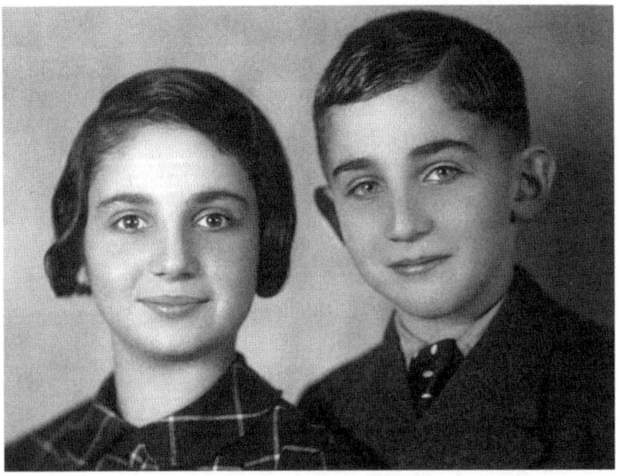

17. Ella and Paul, Always Together, Sometime in 1937

Mother really disliked the city water and she insisted that I only bathe in water that would not leave a calcium deposit or soap residue anywhere on my body. This called for additional scrubbing as well as an elaborate rinsing procedure. The bathing routine always culminated in the cutting and shaping of toenails and fingernails.

Sister

As I have said, I have an older sister named Ella. Besides me, she is the only survivor of our immediate family. She still lives in Trenčín. She never left that town except for the time she spent in the Ravensbruck labor camp in 1944 and 1945.

Ella inherited all of my mother's best characteristics. She has always been helpful, hardworking and considerate of others. It was my sister who first encouraged me to join the Hashomer Hatzair (The Youth Guard), a Zionist organization that was part of the international scouting movement.[6]

And it was she who continually warned me to behave myself, as I was always on the verge of being discovered as the instigator of some mischief or other. Even though we shared a tiny bedroom for several years and it was she who always tidied up the mess I left, our lives were very separate. I became particularly jealous of her when she reached the age of seventeen and several young men started courting her. I can still recall the pranks I pulled to discourage them, such as sending Gejza Fabian (who was to become her husband) on senseless errands.

18. My Dearest Sister Ella, 1940

During the war, Ella kept very much to herself and we saw very little of each other. After 1942, I was a student and spent most of my time with my Lutheran friends, whereas she had a clerical job that kept her quite busy. She maintained her connections with young Jewish men and women, many of whom had adopted assumed names and gone into hiding. Ella helped them in various ways, often acting as a courier to pro-

[6]Hashomer Hatzair was founded through the merger of two Jewish youth groups (Hashomer and Zeíirei Zion) in Galicia, Austria-Hungary in 1913. The political wing of the group was moderate, advocating a bi-national approach to the Jewish-Arab standoff in Palestine. The organization boasted 70,000 members in 1939, primarily centered in Eastern Europe. The group remains active today and is now based in Israel, though it sponsors programs worldwide.

vide them with much-needed money. Such activity was of course strictly forbidden. I suspect that with her quiet and unassuming ways, she had everyone fooled.

When she was finally betrayed in October 1944, she was shipped first to the Sered concentration camp (fifty-five kilometers northeast of Bratislava) and then to Germany. Her life was spared by getting assigned as a slave laborer in a factory where salvaged parts from downed Luftwaffe airplanes were cleaned and reconditioned for subsequent recycling as spare parts. The expendable Jewish girls had to scour the metal components with highly-corrosive solvents without the benefit of gloves or protective garments. They were only Jews, after all.

As the Soviet Army approached from the east, the laborers at her factory were ordered to evacuate, and so began the ordeal that came to be known as the "death march." By this time Ella was starving and so sick it would only be a matter of time before she would have to stop and rest—and receive the inevitable bullet meted out to all stragglers. Almost miraculously, she was saved by two of her childhood friends who shared their tiny portion of food with her and propped her up when her feet buckled beneath her.

The column of emaciated refugees became disorganized and dispersed, and when she and her friends heard an approaching artillery bombardment while they were passing through a section of forest, they stealthily drifted away from the others. Somehow, they managed to survive in the woods for those final days until liberation.

Ella returned to Trenčín, where she discovered I too had survived. She did her best to make a home for us both, but I had already set my sights on a new life in America. Despite my attempts to run him off, Gejza reappeared and won my sister's heart; they married and now have two children (both of whom are physicians) and four grandchildren.

But her suffering did not end with the liberation. Under the Communist regime, she was reduced to holding a menial clerical position with no hope of advancement and was exposed to all of the deprivations common to a police state. She managed to cope with all of life's hardships by preserving a sharp mind, a friendly attitude for everyone, and a stoic disposition. When we talk about sorrows, past or present, she always finishes the conversation by reminding me, "You cannot do much about that."

To this day she is, and will always remain, my dearest friend.

Grandfather Strassmann

Father was the son of an innkeeper, Filip Strassmann, who invested whatever money he could in my father's education. I do not remember much of him since he always kept to himself on account of his heart condition (I recall him popping nitroglycerin pills). Grandfather smoked an old-fashioned long-stemmed pipe that descended from his lip all the way to his belt. It smelled terrible.

The oldest child, Filip had two brothers and one sister. His original homeplace was in the village of Strelnica, on the border between Slovakia and Bohemia. For many years he lived in Horny Lideč, where he owned the inn. He also moonlighted as administrative manager of a local nobleman's estate. Before the outbreak of the First World War, Grandfather Strassmann moved to Trenčín and acquired another inn in what was then the poorest district of town, known as Alsovaros.

Grandmother Anna, whose maiden name was Ziegler, was born in Beluša. Her family lived there until their deportation in 1942. Anna's brother, Fero, had four sons and a daughter. Three of the Ziegler boys survived the war. One fled to England in 1939 and fought in the British Army, while another obtained forged papers and managed to pass through those terrible times without being fingered as a Jew. How the third son, Ferdinand, survived nobody knows; he suddenly appeared in Poprad in March of 1945 as a political officer in the Czechoslovak forces that came from the Soviet Union.

One of Anna's sisters, Hanna, married a gentile farmer from a nearby village against the will of her parents. The Ziegler family never spoke of her or saw her again, as her marriage to a gentile (and a peasant at that) was considered a great shame for a Jewish family. My sister discovered this "skeleton in the closet" by accident many years after Hanna had passed away.

During the Great War, Grandfather Filip attained a level of prosperity that enabled him to purchase a fine house on the main square in the center of Trenčín. My sister Ella and her children, Thomas and Zuzka (Susan), still own this house.

Grandfather Filip was exceedingly frugal; perhaps this contributed to his economic rise. The man would hand-deliver mail to save on postage. I was told that he once walked, during an especially hard winter, over fifty miles to return money owed. Grandfather Weiner—who was perpetually poor—always treated me to some special sweets from the local Turkish hawker every Saturday after prayers, but I do not recall ever having received a single gift from Grandfather Filip. Grandmother Anna made up for it by giving me her delicious baked potato skins with fried onions—it is still my favorite meal.

My paternal grandmother Anna, or "*malka*" (which means "small" in Slovak), came from a large clan; someone was always visiting someone. One of these families came to live with (or near) us when they were dispossessed of their property in 1940. But after the deportations started in 1942, my father could not protect them any more and they all ultimately perished. I sorely missed my Uncle Kling, a mechanical genius who taught me how to repair electrical outlets and the fuses that frequently shorted out.

During the period from 1942 through September 1944, my paternal grandparents were protected by my father's "Presidential Exemption," also known as the "white card."[7] Such fragile immunity wouldn't last forever, and in early in September 1944, my grandparents were deported to the notorious Auschwitz labor camp in Poland, where they ultimately perished along with so many others.

Grandfather Weiner

As a boy, my favorite family member by far was my maternal grandfather, Alexander "Dedko" Weiner. He spent more time with me than anyone else in the family, especially after the outside world began to close in on us in 1938. He was one of the few Jewish craftsmen who made

---

[7]For more information regarding the "Presidential Exemption," see Part III, page 155.

very fine cabinetry, often ornamented with rich veneer inlays of rare and beautiful woods. Orders for such furniture were often placed years ahead of expected delivery, and many items were procured to become part of a girl's dowry. This provided a somewhat predictable due date, as girls were generally engaged to be married by the time they turned twenty.

Dedko had an optimistic outlook on life. Whenever someone brought bad news (which was becoming an alarmingly frequent occurrence), he was about the only person who was sure to shrug and say, "It could be worse." He liked to sing or hum Yiddish songs while he worked. He closed down his shop in 1935 and moved in with us, occupying a tiny room in the attic of our house and taking on the thankless job of yard supervisor; it was his charge to make sure merchandise was not pilfered. He also saw to it that I attended prayers every Saturday and all major holidays without exception. We used to visit the carpentry shop of his former apprentice, Molnar; Dedko enjoyed overseeing the delicate process of applying layers of varnish to the fine woods. Since the smell of lacquer and turpentine was intense, Dedko and Molnar used to help themselves to ample doses of strong plum brandy "to counter the vapors"—for "medicinal purposes," you might say.

After 1940, curfews were imposed that severely restricted our movements. Since we couldn't go out very much, Dedko set up a small workshop area in his tiny room and taught me the art of making fine veneer inlays. We started with small wooden jewelry boxes. I developed—and still retain—an enormous appreciation of the craftsmanship that goes into the production of handcrafted items that feature intricate inlays of wood or stone.

Grandfather's reputation as a master craftsman saved him from deportation to a death camp in 1942. Instead, he was transported to the slave labor camp at Nováky that was operated by the Slovak fascists as a business enterprise for the benefit of high-ranking Hlinka Guard officials. One of the specialties of this camp was the manufacture of custom furniture. I was told by one of the surviving inmates that Dedko was admired for his cheerful disposition and conviction that a liberating messiah would miraculously appear at any moment. Dedko had the reputation of always looking for the good when everyone else was despondent. I am sure he

19. Grandmother Emma Weiner

went to his death with expectations of deliverance from all of the woes of this earth. When somebody brings me bad news, I will always hear my grandfather saying, "It could be worse."

Grandmother Weiner

I do not recall much about my maternal grandmother Emma (whose maiden name was Diamant) except that when I was about three years old I came to visit her while she was resting in bed. She was very pale and the visit was a short one. I was told that this would be the last time I would see her. Emma was much respected as a wise woman. She had a tiny store selling embroidery patterns at one of the best locations in town. My grandmother not only sold the patterns, but also tutored the girls in how to improve the quality and complexity of their embroidery.

Her additional income came from being a highly respected marriage broker. How this came about offers an interesting insight into the Jewish community life of her era. As in all societies, birth, marriage, and burial were the monumental life events for every family. Of these, marriage was perhaps most important, because it involved an element of choice in an environment largely constrained by custom and economics. Picking the right marriage partner was often a key to a family's rise in status and prosperity. Dowries and inheritance played an important role in prenuptial negotiations; for a girl to be married into the "right" family was paramount. It was often one of the principal topics of chitchat in the synagogue and the coffeehouse.

In preparation for marriage, and as part of the social pressure to follow traditional mores, a girl had to start making her trousseau as soon as she entered school. That involved learning needlework and embroidery based on patterns sold in one of the many handicraft shops in town. I do not think that my grandmother Emma's shop was much bigger than a hundred square feet, but it was filled with wooden trays bearing copper metal patterns embossed with fashionable designs of the day. Here's how it worked: A girl's mother would bring in a piece of linen, and my grandmother would imprint the pattern on it using water soluble blue ink and those copper pattern templates. After practicing various stitches on this scrap piece, the girl would show her work to my grandmother and hopefully receive her approval to begin work on her trousseau. She would often complete some simple border work on bed sheets and pillowcases before attempting the more intricate designs necessary for the trousseau.

My grandmother was very much in love with my grandfather. During the First World War, Emma lived alone in Budapest. She was told—quite incorrectly—that her husband had been killed at the front. She went into severe shock and suffered afterward from a weakened heart, a condition that hastened her passing in 1932.

The Matchmaker

The process of developing the manual dexterity necessary for executing this intricate embroidery consumed untold hundreds of hours of diligent practice. As the complexity of the work increased, completing it well called for intelligence, a good eye for close work, and industriousness. Observing this developmental pattern provided my grandmother with the ability to predict a girl's spousal aptitude as accurately as any formal test then available. Therefore, Emma's judgment was frequently decisive when the relative merits of bridal candidates were being considered during the matrimonial negotiations.

Of course, my grandmother made sure that her only daughter, Frances, was suitably prepared to be the most attractive prospect for the most desirable suitor then available in the town. That was my father, a former military officer and one of the few Jews in the neighborhood with higher education. I do not know any of the details about how the marriage was brokered, though I doubt very much that my father could have been talked into anything he had not decided to do anyway.

Years later, two women from Trenčín told me they could have been my mother had it not been for the unfair advantage leveraged by that "schemer from the embroidery shop." My sister vehemently denies this story, yet I find it a plausible explanation for why two assertive, determined (and rich, but not terribly bright) women did not stand a chance against Emma!

The emphasis placed on learning and intelligence over mere material wealth offers a partial explanation for the propensity of Jews to favor intellectual pursuits. Tradition dictated that even if he was poor, a learned young Jewish man was a preferable mate for a girl from a good family—that led to a matriarchal society. It didn't take me long to figure that out when I myself (a penniless man) married into the prominent Rosenthal family (of Maidenform bra fame) in 1954. The entire clan showed up for the wedding and was visibly delighted to see one of their own marrying a poor, but promising, European import.

The Strassmann Business

My father's rapid rise in business was reflected in the new residence and commercial building he built in 1934 in the midst of the Great Depression. The roofline was forty-five feet above street level; the building was 135 feet long and occupied an entire city block. The storefront proudly announced that the Strassmann firm offered "Diversified Merchandise in Retail and Wholesale—Fertilizer, Feed and Agricultural Supplies."

Solidly constructed of reinforced concrete, the compound included an apartment (our residence), business offices, warehouses, our retail store and an additional storefront that was rented out to generate income, and the shipping and receiving yard. Quite ahead of its time, the flat roof of the warehouse was covered in topsoil and sported an expansive lawn and garden! We grew strawberries, flowers, and some shrubs in the garden while the lawn was a favorite spot to relax and sunbathe (though I preferred to build tented "fortresses" out of blankets there).

In the classic style, there was a large gate and passageway alongside the store through which trucks and the farmers' carts entered the yard for loading and deliveries. I also recall a heavy steel door next to the store entrance that led to the basement, where we stored goods that required a cool, dry environment.

Our living quarters were above the commercial areas. Three rooms—the living room (which was rarely used), dining room, and my parents' bedroom—faced the street, while the two children's bedrooms faced the terrace. The kitchen and the cook's quarters looked out onto the yard.

20. Business Storefront. Family Apartment Upstairs.

There were many delays during the construction, as the architect found it difficult to supervise the contractors, and my father had to frequently intervene to break the logjam. The architect, a man named Silberstein, was touted for his designs of public buildings. He also designed the custom cabinetry for our living room and dining room. My sister managed to salvage a few of these fine pieces, and they are still in service in her small one-bedroom apartment in Trenčín.

Sadly, the building was razed in the 1960s to make way for a theater and entertainment complex for the Slovak Army. But with the Communists gone, it is now used for public concerts and other events.

Father's rise as a leading merchant in the district can be traced to his innovative approach to financing his distribution channels. He established a chain of retail distributors in the surrounding villages, each operated by a war veteran he knew he could trust. He cemented these relationships by supplying kerosene to the local villages, which was a very smart move; that's how the Strassmann firm became the regional agent for Standard Oil of New York. As many as a hundred barrels of this highly inflammable stuff were stored in the basement underneath the warehouse, just a few yards from our bedrooms.

Father also introduced the use of nitrate-based fertilizer to the district to increase agricultural yields. At times there was enough nitrate of ammonia stacked up in the yard to blow the neighborhood sky-high. Our firm also imported high-quality flour from the USA in varieties that were not available from local mills. I recall that we supplied local housewives with the popular semolina flour from Nebraska.

In a two-decade period, my father and mother (who was the cashier, treasurer and personnel manager) built up a business that flourished and expanded steadily until 1938. I believe that my father was able to succeed because of his commercial education, whereas his primary competitors (the Fursts, who had been in the business for more than a century) were just relaxing and not innovating. My father's prosperity was largely driven by the pleasure he got from engaging in risky commercial concepts. For example, he once tried to corner the market on a product made of prunes that was used to sweeten steamed dumplings (a mainstay of the peasant diet). Every fall, he bought a carload of prunes at exceptionally low prices from Bosnia, and for one reason or another, there was always something wrong with them. My mother always chided him about it, saying that bargains do not pay off.

Because of my father's efforts to enhance the commercial affairs in the district, he was respected as one of the leading citizens in town—he was in fact the first Jew elected to the district council. This body was a regulatory committee that governed commercial regulations; it functioned under the auspices of the town government by virtue of grants of privileges dating back to medieval times. After the war, I was grandfathered in to the council because of my father's exalted reputation, though I had no real commercial experience—I was Adko Strassmann's son, and that was good enough.

In spite of his notable business acumen, Father was not a very gregarious sort. Some of the other merchants resented the fact that he didn't patronize the coffeehouses, the favorite gathering place for local dealmakers and gossipmongers. Years later, I was told that I was just like my father—always walking faster than anyone thought proper in a conservative society that did not court change.

I think that my father's outlook was much more cosmopolitan than that of other merchants, Jewish or otherwise. The sign on our store included the phrase "Merchants in Colonial Wares," which meant that we sold a variety of imported goods. Our store offered camphor from India (for home remedies), tea from Ceylon, cloves from Java (of ceremonial use during Jewish and Catholic holidays), cinnamon from Madagascar, sardines from Portugal, semolina flour from Nebraska, kerosene from Baku (on the Caspian Sea), fertilizer from Chile, and coffee from Brazil. In today's supermarkets such variety is commonplace; in a provincial town in Czechoslovakia in the middle of the Depression, such luxuries were truly remarkable.

One of Father's great adventures was his one and only visit to London and Brussels in the early 1930s. I remember that our bookshelves were filled with travelogues, including the complete works of Sven Hedin, the explorer who wrote about Central Asia. My father also harbored a dream that he would one day own a place with a large garden, somewhere in a land of peace and tolerance—which to him meant England. In such a setting, his children and grandchildren could attend the best universities and speak English.

As I look out beyond my computer to the meadow that stretches beyond my window, I often think that this is exactly what my father had in mind: a life far from Trenčín—even before the bad times began.

Relatives

I was always aware that relatives were important because much of the life and conversation revolved about their lives and troubles, of which there were always plenty, especially as their dependency on my father grew. They were certainly a colorful lot.

Though Jews were generally not engaged in the engineering profession, I developed during my childhood the fixed idea that this was what I wished to be. There was cousin Karol Schalk, who was completing his studies in mechanical engineering in Prague. There were also vague references to the eastern branch of the Strassmann family, in which Moritz Strassmann held the position as supervisory engineer on the staff of the Hungarian Railroad. Many years later, his nephew gave me a medal that was awarded to Moritz for his services in the construction of a number of railroad tunnels between Hungary and the Ukraine.

Perhaps the most colorful Strassmann relative was Erwin Soos, whom I discovered after the war living in Aachen, Germany. According to Erwin, his mother was a sister of Moritz Strassmann. Against the opposition of all relatives, she married Soos's father, who was then the political commissar of the abortive Kun Communist revolt in 1919. Soos was executed when the uprising failed. A monument to honor him was erected in Košice, Slovakia, after the end of World War II.

Like his father, Erwin was a dedicated Communist and he served the party as editor of one of the leading Slovak Communist news organs. He later became head of the Czechoslovak foreign broadcasting news services. His luck ultimately ran out and he was imprisoned during one of the many Soviet purges, but thanks to his family's long service to the party, he was generously allowed to go into voluntary exile in Germany rather than rotting in a cell or being carted off to a gulag in Siberia. He spent the remainder of his life in deep bitterness. In addition to receiving a small pension from the German government (as a former slave laborer), he supported himself by analyzing the contents of several dozen Communist newspapers for the global strategic analysis firm, Oxford Analytica. During the Cold War his work served as a useful source of information for the Western intelligence services. Such analysis was often performed by émigrés, who knew how to interpret the meager news that was being published behind the Iron Curtain.

LIFE

It is alleged in some historical summaries that Jewish merchants were present in Trenčín at the end of the second century C.E., when the town was little more than a Roman military post and Jews served as intermediaries in the trade between Romans and the Germanic tribes.

In 1938, about 89,000 Jews lived in Slovakia. Some 10,000 lived in the territory ceded to Hungary in 1940 (in Ruthenia and sub-Carpathia), while the remainder made up about 3 percent of the Slovak population. Slovakia was poorer and far less industrialized than the Czech crown provinces of Bohemia and Moravia, and so were its Jews. They were engaged mostly in retail trade. A small number of Jews provided a large share of the legal and medical services as well.

The Jewish Community

There are no records about Slovakian Jewish communities in the early medieval era, except for a brief mention of a trading group in the eleventh century in Komarno, about seventy kilometers south of Trenčín. There was a large influx of Jews into Slovakia after their suppression in Bohemia in the twelfth century. The earliest records of a Jewish community in Trenčín date to 1663, when a large number migrated to the area seeking freedom from persecution in Moravia. The first Trenčín rabbi was apparently a man named Israel Chaijim, who officiated over a rustic wood-framed synagogue in 1791. That building burned down, but ultimately, the Jewish community erected an imposing replacement that opened its doors in September of 1913. It was taken over by the state in 1990. The huge central room is now empty and forlorn, following several unsuccessful attempts by the local government to convert it into a cultural center. Today, it stands as a memorial to the Jews of Trenčín who were murdered during the Holocaust.

21. The Synagogue, about 1929

Before the Second World War, the Trenčín Jewish community was fully equipped to sustain its religious customs and traditions. It had a burial society, Chevra Kadischa, to perform the ritual functions for the dead, and there was a Jewish almshouse and a cemetery, which is now the only Jewish institution remaining in Trenčín. The community operated a ritual bath, or *mikva*, and supported a ritual butcher and slaughterhouse. There was a kosher meal service for the poor, a kosher hotel with a dining room, and a Jewish elementary school was established in 1800. In the 1930s, the school had over 130 pupils. The community also supported a thriving assortment of volunteer groups; in the prewar years, these organizations became increasingly concentrated on supporting Zionist movements, especially for the youth, most prominent among them being the Hashomer Hatzair.

The Jewish community of Trenčín consisted of about 2,000 souls out of a population of about 19,000. It congregated in the large synagogue that even today is one of the largest public buildings in town. That is not remarkable since the Jewish merchants and legal or medical professionals provided much of the trade and services to perhaps as many as fifty surrounding villages.

The Jewish community was largely self-supporting: It levied taxes (in addition to the state-mandated taxes) to support its own schools, had its own charities, ritual baths, and the synagogue with a seating capacity of about a thousand. The synagogue had a very rigid hierarchy: Women were seated on the balcony, which had separate entrances from the street, while their menfolk prayed on the ground floor. Young boys were permitted to visit their mothers on the balcony, but the little girls were discouraged from descending the stairs to visit their fathers. The wealthy merchants "owned" permanent seats in the temple (a status symbol for which they offered substantial donations), with the more generous donors receiving the prime locations. Absence from services, especially on high holidays, always resulted in community disapproval. My family's pew was in a less grand location, because Grandfather Filip did not believe that proximity to the lectern made any difference to God (or perhaps he was simply too frugal to see the value in such an investment). My father felt that the local rabbi was incompetent, an opinion shared by everyone in the community, though only Father voiced it in public.

Community life was anchored on the Jewish parochial school (the first five elementary grades) and the synagogue. There were many holidays to observe. Adhering to the old Jewish religious ways did not make much sense to the increasingly radicalized Zionist youth. What particularly grated on us was that the liturgy and prayers were performed exclusively in Hebrew. I didn't understand any of it, with the minor exception of familiar phrases. The Jewish teachers did not teach us to actually understand Hebrew, although we had to memorize long passages—an exercise which I suppose was good training for future learning. Ironically, it was those same anticlerical Zionists who later insisted that we learn modern Hebrew as a requirement for emigrating to Palestine.

Although he was accepted as one of the leaders of the community (which is to say, he was a generous contributor to charities), my father was highly critical of our rabbi for never mastering Slovak so that his congregation could understand him. In many ways, there was a growing chasm between the youth and the elders. On one hand, the presiding leaders demanded compliance with the orthodox religious observances. On the other, there existed a simmering rebellion against the "old ways" by those who had more secular inclinations. Such sentiments were encouraged by the time I was about seven through my adolescent association with Hashomer Hatzair. This organization was decidedly agnostic, socially conscious, and fervently Zionist. Its leadership flatly rejected the idea of remaining in Slovakia, insisting instead that all Jews should go to Palestine, where free people would live in a utopian communal society.

As conditions worsened, the Zionist platform became more attractive, as their plan offered an escape from the persecution we faced in Slovakia. Hashomer members sang rousing songs that were emotionally uplifting (the singing in the synagogue, such as it was, consisted mostly of morose wailing). The Hashomer singing was militantly energetic and enhanced by a large dose of martial music that was indiscriminately plagiarized from various international sources. I loved to march down the main square belting out an Italian song that made fun of Mussolini. I later learned that many of these political ditties were drawn from the Russian socialist movement (which in turn borrowed some of ours).

The leftist youth always had the best songs and the comeliest girls—both of which were welcome distractions to ideologically more important matters. The inspiring songs and exuberant outdoor activities, such as camping and hiking to exhaustion, offered comfort and a sense of belonging to the youthful rebels as the bad times were closing in.

Domestic Matters

Much of my childhood was occupied with menial tasks such as hauling wood from a deep basement with thirty-six steep steps and on up to the first floor kitchen (twenty-two more steps), or to the second floor laundry (another twenty-two steps). As you can tell, I counted them many times! Twice a year my grandfather purchased a cartload of tree trunks that were cut in six- or eight-foot lengths; they were sold by the local woodcutters on designated market days. These woodsmen dumped the logs in our yard where another team of workers took over and chopped, then split the logs into small pieces that would fit in our stoves.

Market days were always a colorful experience; they were events around which much of the community's commercial and social life revolved. On various days, certain items were featured: some market days were devoted to livestock trading, some to poultry and vegetables, and yet others to clothing and housewares.

In addition to my wood-hauling chores, I was always kept busy picking up blocks of ice from the local ice factory. This plant produced ice from the town's water supply. Most of the local housewives obtained their ice from the local butchers, who maintained their own icehouses. Their ice was harvested directly from the polluted river in winter and stored under an insulating blanket of sawdust. The river froze solid where it passed through Trenčín just about every year. Keeping meat refrigerated with such tainted ice was certainly not very sanitary. My mother used this situation to justify the strict kosher dietary rules; it seemed sensible enough to me. One of the principal causes of chronic disease in Slovakia was a stomach ulcer resulting from spoiled food and too much alcohol.

The water supply in the villages came mostly from local wells that could not be isolated from the effluents seeping in from barns housing livestock and even from outhouses. Actual sewer systems were only in use in the major towns. The average life expectancy was about fifty-five years for townsfolk and (not surprisingly) even less for the peasants. Anyone over sixty-five was considered positively ancient (and probably an invalid). Women aged much faster than the men; women in their thirties looked old and haggard. In their ubiquitous somber black clothing and matching headscarves they were quite an unattractive sight.

The villagers were very poor but kept amazingly neat houses. But it was a different story out on the hillsides. The high mortality rate coupled with the emigration of many men resulted in a population of desperately impoverished castoffs and widows who occupied miserable little one-room log cabins. *Partizáns* would be taken in and cared for when wounded or laid low by the severe winter weather. Caring for a debilitated *partizán* had the added advantage of filling the cramped space of a mountain cottage with an armed occupant at times when soldiers, deserters, escaped POWs, and even Nazi turncoats were drifting through the mountain settlements seeking food, shelter, and anything else they could get. When my health failed late in January 1945, I was taken in by an old woman (now I'm wondering how "old" she really was) who for a few days fed me with milk, noodles, and farm cheese; along with others, she cared for me until I recovered my strength. That was truly an unselfish act of charity, because harboring a *partizán* was punishable by death. I had no money to offer her, only fleas.

Customs

In my youth, kosher guidelines were always carefully and meticulously followed. Together with my schoolmates, I attended the obligatory morning services every Saturday. They were held in the largest classroom in the Jewish school rather than the cavernous synagogue, which was reserved for more formal services.

The synagogue was a substantial building; it employed the latest reinforced concrete construction techniques, though the fanciful architecture reflected the ornate Byzantine style. A wonderful central cupola capped the building. Particularly devout elders used a separate small room annexed to the main building as a tabernacle for prayers. My grandfather Weiner saw to it that I attended weekly services without fail; he viewed it as a community obligation. Children with musical talent were chosen to sing the leading parts of the program, usually incorporating Eastern European liturgy or local variants of folk songs. In due course the soloists developed their own unique variations on a theme, and it was always a source of great amusement to witness the effect of a new musical embellishment on the disapproving eyes and ears of the conservative elders, who of course preferred the old-fashioned wailing.

Vera Suess was the lead soprano (and a bit of a showoff). She was the daughter of a textile merchant in our neighborhood, and I had a bad crush on her since the age of five. My principal rival for her favors (such as sharing a chicken liver sandwich) was Palo "Ravid" Ringwald. In spite of our romantic rivalry, we have remained lifelong friends. He now lives in kibbutz Dalia in Israel, and I visit him whenever I can. He likes to remind me that when he was eight, he nearly blinded me by plunging a pen into my right eye as we quarreled over who would share their lunch with Vera. Franco Goldner, the lead baritone, also remains a good friend to this day. He settled in Gothenburg, Sweden, and I visit with him either by phone or in person at least once a year. I can still see the faces of these and many other classmates (though I admit that my memory is refreshed by the obligatory annual class photographs).

The town of Trenčín honored me as a "Distinguished Citizen" in 1995. During an interview with the mayor I was asked what I thought of the town now. I told him that when I walk the streets, I see ghosts everywhere. In my mind's eye, I saw the faces of my friends and neighbors from before the war peeping out of windows and doorways as I walked the streets. Most didn't survive the Holocaust.

22. The Faces I Remember to This Day, 1941

Religious Observance

By today's standards, our mode of worship was quite strict; still, I must say that there was a faction in Trenčín who considered the rest of us improperly secular, as we did not adopt the distinctive clothing and other trappings of orthodox Jews, such as side locks and ritualistic underwear.

My chief complaint with the "old ways" was the fact that the liturgy was in Hebrew; it was arcane and incomprehensible, and totally ill adapted to the concerns of modern Jewish life. While I followed the required routines with great care and was able to recite long passages from memory, I did not understand much of what I was saying; for prayers to be considered acceptable, one only had to pronounce the words correctly. Only later did I pick up a smattering of the Hebrew language. Even then the prayers did not make much sense to me, especially the unceasing pleadings. Later, I came to understand why I was to inherit the burdens of centuries of persecution and tears.

Sabbath was observed. The candles were lit on Friday night and my mother blessed the challah, a traditional braided bread. The Seder was an important ritual feast that was not overlooked, nor did we truncate the prescribed Haggadah liturgy—we went through the whole text while waiting for a truly sumptuous feast that included wine, the only time I was ever allowed to touch the beverage. The wine was not particularly good, having been supplied by the rabbinical monopoly. Perhaps for this reason I still do not drink wine! It seems that our likes and dislikes are formed much earlier than our parents suspect.

One of the most memorable events for me was the administration of an annual ritual by Grandfather Weiner. The day before Yom Kippur, orthodox Jews perform a rite called *kapores*. This ceremony involves the sacrifice of a chicken to remind man what he deserves to receive for his sins against God, although my grandfather insisted (much to my father's dismay) that the real purpose was to ward off evil—a sort of talisman. The whole process does have certain pagan overtones: Before the slaughter, the live (and frantically screaming) cock is swung over the head of the oldest male child three times. A prayer is then recited and the animal is killed according to kosher law with a swift chop to the neck with an ax. Years later, when I had to dart across a road that was under machine-gun fire, I had the ridiculous idea that I could not be hit because of *kapores*. I also discovered that anthropologists studying aboriginal tribal customs—including in voodoo incantations—have often witnessed various forms of this ritual. Perhaps my three male grandchildren would benefit from this supplemental "life insurance" policy, although I am sure that my American-born wife would consider it to be an unacceptable form of primitive superstition.

One's religious foundation is generally not the result of some theological discourse, it is a habit drawn from the prosaic patterns of family rituals experienced during childhood. For instance, for me, matzo balls in chicken soup convey a memory of my mother's solemn pronouncement (always uttered in the same tone and with the identical timing) during the Passover feast that this year the soup is "*nicht schoen, aber gut,*" meaning "not pretty, but good." Why this phrase has stuck with me for all these years I cannot explain, but it still bears a magical memory imprint.

Religious injunctions also prompted theological experimentation. One day, Franco Goldner and I were thoroughly bored with the daylong religious services during the mandatory fasting on Yom Kippur. As I recall, it was on a Saturday when transgressions earned double demerits in one's personal accounting ledger in Heaven. This double-entry bookkeeping arrangement was my childhood understanding of religion, ethics, and justice. Accordingly, if sins exceeded good deeds, your accounts would be transferred to Hell after you died. Franco and I figured that eating a small piece of pork sausage would be the most formidable way of testing the Laws. And so we indulged, but there was no thunder or lightning. Both of us felt badly about it after the fact, and we still remembered the incident when we met in Sweden forty years later.

Language and Culture

Until I entered school at the age of six, much of the conversation at home was in German, because that was the language in which my father conducted many of his commercial dealings with manufacturer's representatives who called on us from the large commercial centers of Bratislava, Brno, Prague, and Vienna. We enjoyed entertaining these traveling salesmen, as they were a wonderful source of news, gossip, and commercial intelligence.

They became personal friends and were treated to lunch and sometimes dinner at our table. As salespeople, they were typically extroverts and exuberantly optimistic. They incessantly prodded Father to expand his business—it was in their best interest, after all. Unfortunately, they also turned out to be an unreliable source of intelligence about the severity of the threat posed by Hitler. Having learned my lesson the hard way, I never take the recommendations of a commission-based salesman at face value.

With the solid record of success predicated on rapid growth and his willingness to seize opportunities others overlooked, I think it was my father's inclination to embrace good news over bad that ultimately worked against us. This optimistic mindset led him to discount the mounting risks of staying on in Slovakia until it was too late. I later discovered that Father started buying properties at bargain prices from a number of Jews who were liquidating their assets in 1935. That's how my father, in partnership with Andor Kubiček, owner of the town's largest drugstore, wound up owning a large factory for making bricks and acquired well over a hundred acres of pasture and arable land. The writing was on the wall—he just refused to see it.

Until I left for school, my family always employed governesses. These caregivers were usually widows, divorcees, or otherwise unencumbered older ladies. Most were German-speaking non-Jewish women who moved on from family to family as the children outgrew the need for constant supervision. My earliest experiences with the military were the result of my favorite governess, Ottie, who was younger and better looking than most of the women in her profession. She had a certain attraction for men in uniform. Ottie often arranged excursions for "fresh air" that somehow managed to take us wherever the soldiers were conducting their training exercises. The enlisted men were ordered to keep me entertained by allowing me to watch them set up their weapons (which I enjoyed immensely) while the officers were taking good care of Ottie. I cried and cried when the fun-loving Ottie was summarily dismissed by my angry father for (I figured out years later) fraternizing with the officers. It seems she had developed "female problems," and that topic was strictly forbidden from discussion "in front of the children" (though I was painfully curious about this mystery).

Family

My father was considered the patriarch of the family. Though he was no mafia don, it was only after seeing the movie *The Godfather* that I began to understand some of the intricacies of my own family dynamics, as well as the power of his patronage over an extended network of shopkeepers who depended on his good will (and financing) to stay in business.

Father had three sisters. They all married men who kept tiny retail food shops. The closest relatives were Aunt Pavla Altmann in Trenčín (with one daughter, Alice), Aunt Erna Schalk in Košeca (with son Karol, daughter Elizabeth, and grandchild Ivan), and Aunt Irma Flack in Puchov (with son Josef). There were repeated visitations to and from the family for birthdays, anniversaries, and whenever help was needed, which was often. Much time could be filled up just keeping track of who visited whom, and how often. I remember spending several summers with the aunts in the villages and getting to know my cousins, especially Karol, who was studying engineering in Prague.

Most of the clan was economically dependent on my father. That kept things pretty tense, though the only real quarrel I can recall involved my mother's only brother, Eugen "Bubbi" Weiner, a revolver-toting speculator from Prague, who refused to pay my father back for a rather large loan.

In the 1930s, there was no organized social welfare system in Slovakia. The extended family depended on the wealthiest relative for support in hard times. Although I distinctly remember that my parents obtained passports and exit visas in 1938, the idea of leaving all the dependent relatives to fend for themselves was something my father would never do. He was a man of honor to whom family came before all else.

My mother always worked side-by-side with my father, keeping the same long hours. She was a working mother, as was typical of Jewish families. Grandfather Alexander also worked in the store in the morning, checking out outgoing merchandise as it was loaded onto the trucks and then again in the evening, when the trucks rolled into the yard with the inevitable returns.

After 1939, as the village stores of our relatives were closed down one by one, some of our uncles came to live with us and worked wherever Father could find employment for them. However, as temporary residents, they were all swept away by the first wave of deportations that started in the spring of 1942.

Education

The Jewish school in Trenčín was a parochial school; that is, it was funded entirely by a Jewish community tax on the parents, based on their ability to pay rather than the number of children. The school had three classrooms and three teachers. The first classroom was for the first two grades and was taught by Mr. Brunner, who held that position for more than thirty years and was considered a trusted mentor and advisor to several generations of pupils.

The second classroom was for the third grade. This class was taught by Mr. Santo, who was a little senile (we called him "no-see-no-hear Santo"). He enforced strict discipline by means of a bamboo rod laid smartly across the knuckles of one's outstretched hand. I recall being a frequent target of Mr. Santo's switch, especially after being caught distributing condoms to my snickering classmates, who found the entire performance a wonderful break from the tedium of their lessons.

The third classroom was for the fourth, fifth, and sixth grades. That is where the real education began, though the turnover among the teachers was very high. I was lucky, because my father managed to convince Josef Weiser to come and teach in Trenčín. Weiser was a refugee from east Slovakia, subsequently the editor of Pravda and Dean of the School of Journalism in the post-Communist regime until he was purged. I credit Weiser for my love of history as a means of understanding contemporary affairs. He held the class spellbound for hours by making history come alive as an oft-repeated tragedy.

I remember the last week before the school was closed for good in early in 1942. Weiser colorfully described the destruction of Jerusalem by the Romans. The electricity for the school had been already cut off. The teacher shared his highly descriptive and dramatic narrative with us on this wintry February afternoon. The class did not move a muscle nor make a sound, although the room was ultimately plunged into complete darkness. I still visit Mr. Weiser whenever possible to acknowledge my profound debt to him. Good teachers are rare gems, but more valuable.

The school had a tiny room that was advertised as a "gymnasium" that was run by a local branch of the Makabi athletic association. I was more interested in rough-and-tumble street games, such as our local version of rugby. Everyone above the age of ten could participate. Teams were usually chosen by lot, with the smaller boys being sprinkled in among the big lads (who of course scored most of the goals). Each "goal" was a space between two columns on the outer walls of the castle. Once in a while the older girls joined for an enjoyable game that included full-contact tackle. The schoolyard was covered with crushed stone; I believe that over several years, it must have consumed at least a square foot of the skin from my knees and elbows.

Our favorite occupation was to play "cops and robbers" through the cellars and bastions of the ancient fortress. The cops wore a blue cloth armband on their right arm, while the robbers sported a red ribbon on their left. Years later I found out that in the US Army's war games, the "blues" are always the "good guys" and the "reds" are the so-called "aggressor force" (a thinly-veiled reference to the Soviets from the Cold War days). Our game consisted of catching up with either a cop or robber and "killing" them by yanking off their armband. Considering that some of the chase took place on top of crumbling walls that bordered deep pits, it is a miracle that no one was ever maimed in our spirited scuffles.

Anti-Semitism

As a child, almost all of my social contacts were naturally with my classmates. From time to time, my father took me visiting the surrounding villages where his men had stores for distribution of Strassmann merchandise. I also got to know the families of my father's chief assistants. I always had a great deal of exposure to people outside of the Jewish community, which was unusual. But on a more personal level, most of my childhood relationships were with my Jewish peers.

My little group of friends was very tightly knit. We spent many hours carousing and swimming in the river that flowed through Trenčín. As it was something of an open sewer whose dangers were augmented by wicked rapids and sharp stones, it probably wasn't such a good idea. But it seemed much more adventurous to a group of young boys than the chlorinated public swimming pool (from which we were excluded in any case).

At the bends in the river, there was an accumulation of muck through which we often waded. Later, during the war, I learned that even a neglected scratch could fester into a life-threatening wound. Apparently some of the villagers who bathed in this cesspool died of tetanus.

Once in a while, other children threw stones at us and shouted, "Jew! Jew!" but we considered that as natural as mosquito bites. Until just before the deportations began in 1942, we had few apprehensions about anti-Semitism, because we recognized that we were different and somewhat isolated in our separate world. Only rarely was someone mugged or beaten up. From about the age of seven I was a member of a militant Jewish youth group. We took care of our own and were not intimidated, as we always ran together as an organized pack.

Some time in 1941 or early 1942, after the school was shut down, my father put me to work as an apprentice in a machine shop repairing diesel engines used to drive threshing machines. In this way, I followed the track of those who were preparing for emigration. My father also believed that any educated person should also possess manual skills to fall back on if need be. The crew in the machine shop comprised some pretty rough characters, but they treated me well enough—all except for the local Communist (a Spanish Civil War veteran), who resented me not because I was a Jew, but because my father was a prominent capitalist merchant. This experience taught me that anti-Semitism could be a reflection of differences in socioeconomic class as much as a form of ethnic or religious discrimination. Although I tried to acquire "working class" credentials by volunteering to do jobs nobody else wanted to do, it did not assuage the Communist's dislike. As a matter of fact, when my nemesis became the local deputy Communist Party chairman after the war, he refused to acknowledge my combat record (though he had dodged the anti-Nazi uprising by having been held in the local prison, from which escape was quite easy).

Zionist Utopia

The youth group I joined was the local chapter of Hashomer Hatzair, because my sister Ella was already a member. The group rented a little house in the slum district of Trenčín to use as its headquarters. We had meeting rooms, and in the back there were several bedrooms for members who were preparing for emigration to Israel. An emissary from Israel managed the building. I well recall Akiba Neufeld (now Akiba Nir), who corresponded with me when I became interested in the role of Hashomer Hatzair in the uprising. He was a full-time professional who supervised the activities of the youth and devoted much time to those who were learning a trade. The purpose was to get young people prepared for life in collective settlements in Israel. Those who were learning manual trades—particularly carpentry, the building trades, and repair of agricultural equipment—were apprenticed to small shops in Trenčín.

Hashomer Hatzair pursued a policy of aggressive Zionism. The leadership believed that it would require military action to create and then defend the state of Israel. The purpose of such a state was to establish a purely Jewish community where anti-Semitism would not exist and the persecution of the Jews in exile would disappear. Thus freed from oppression, Jews could start building an existence that would enable them to cultivate a unique culture, without the baggage of always being identified by others as an asocial class. Much of this ideology was laced with utopian concepts about how to build a state that would facilitate the creation of ideal communities, where exploitation of the workers by the owners of the means of production would not occur—that is, a socialist state. I vaguely remember one of the major ideological underpinnings of Hashomer Hatzair: Borochov's "inverted pyramid" schema that attempted to explain why Jews were disliked and persecuted. The Marxist-Zionist Borochov maintained that every nation should rely on workers, artisans, and peasants as the basis of state power (the base of the pyramid); intellectuals and business types should be confined to a narrow "superstructure" of the state (the pinnacle of the pyramid). This view mirrored the writings of many utopians who believed that there would be no exploitation of the workers in a just state; the majority of the citizens would in fact comprise the "laboring classes."

After years of studying the structure of organizations, I have come to the conclusion that Hashomer's utopian assumptions were completely wrongheaded. Historically, societies that grew and prospered evolved in exactly the opposite direction of the model embraced by the Hashomer brain trust. Those who were preaching about the dominance of the workers proceeded to amass power for themselves. I have spent a quarter of a century researching the subject and authored several books revealing how the "information workers" who deal in intangibles have supplanted the "workers, farmers, and operators" who deliver tangible products.

While observing the youth revolts of the 1960s, I realized that much of the Hashomer ideology was a blend of counterculture, fear, anticlerical atheism, and backward-looking utopian dreams that failed to grasp the rapid progression of society from an agricultural economy to an industrialized production model and on to the information-based economies of the present. The pastoral communes envisioned for Palestine in the prewar years generated a zeal that can only be found in religious movements. Only by understanding the psychology of the original Zionists can one comprehend the ideas that originally shaped the destiny of Israel. The utopian Zionists had a disproportional influence on the organizations that engineered the creation of the Jewish state in 1948.

The number of ten- to twenty-five-year-olds in Trenčín in the 1930s could not have exceeded a hundred. Nevertheless, just about every ideological faction was represented there. Second to Hashomer (whose membership was about equally divided between boys and girls) was the highly religious Mizrachis (mostly boys), who shied away from sports and aggressive ideas. Then we had the Makabi group, which was devoted to physical prowess and spent most of its time in the tiny local gymnasium. The Makabis of course had the fittest girls (who, I will admit, attracted our attention).

There was also a small right-wing Betar cell in Trenčín. All I remember of them is that they wore black jackboots, broad black belts and brown military-style shirts, and postured just like the Nazi storm troopers. The gossip was that they were acquiring weapons and preparing to seize Palestine by force. Whereas Hashomer lore celebrated the paramilitary Haganah (citizen militia defending communal settlements against marauding Arabs), the Betar ideology was portrayed as being dangerously fascistic.

So as an adolescent, I was introduced to a variety of religious views as well as those of social utopians, communists, and fascists. This wide-ranging exposure to the full spectrum of social constructs inoculated me against the extremism I was about to encounter.

Domesticity

Family life was concentrated in the little time available on weekends or religious holidays. My parents worked from very early in the morning until late in the evening—until the trucks making the rounds of the neighboring villages rolled in and all of the delivered merchandise was accounted for. With few opportunities for extended vacations, this left time only for Sunday or holiday excursions. Once we could afford our own passenger car, we made day trips to the neighboring spas of Trenčíanske Teplice or Pieštany.

23. The Strassmann and Kubiček Families

I do not know why, but most of the photos I have were taken at swimming pools. Here is one taken around 1937 at the Zelena Žaba (Green

Frog) Pool in Trenčianske Teplice. The older woman is Cecilia Kobler, Ilka Kubiček's and Fredi Kobler's mother, a prim, self-righteous lady who always tagged along fully dressed, including her embroidered finery. Standing next to my sister is my old friend, Peter Kubiček.

From time to time we were taken to studios to pose for formal photographs. I did not realize that many of these formal portraits were for passports and visa applications. If there is one regret I have about my family relationships, it is the total absence of communication within the family about what was going on all around us. I suspect my parents were trying to shelter the children from the ugliness of reality, but I also think they were worried about sharing things with me, as I was an assertive, chatty child and might innocently blurt something out at an inopportune moment. Sadly, this communication breakdown persisted to the very end in 1944.

There are few family photos taken after conditions worsened during 1942, culminating with eviction from our home. We could no longer afford the luxury of developing photos and had to give up our camera.

PERIL

My sense that something was amiss began as early as 1936, when I was seven years old, and my worst fears were confirmed within a year. By that time, refugees from Germany had increased from a trickle to a steady stream. Our house served as a way station for people who were collecting money for various causes. My mother was the chairman of the Women's Zionist Organization (WIZO); she was also on every public and private charity list as a generous donor. Andor Kubiček, my father's partner in the brick factory venture, was working with Jewish organizations abroad and was a well-known point of contact for refugees. There was always a heavy flow of traffic passing through our house, as refugees frequently sought support, claiming they needed money for the bribes necessary to finance their flight to Palestine.

Andor was a Slovakian delegate to the Zionist Congress in Basel, Switzerland, in 1939. In addition to having such well-connected sources of intelligence, we heard about what was happening in Germany from our German-Jewish sales reps, many of whom had lost their jobs and were reaching out to their business contacts in hopes of securing assistance. Our own future prospects were never discussed at the dinner table, but I perceived the rising anxiety level.

I remember a particularly poignant incident in which my father's best friend abandoned his wife because he wanted to leave Trenčín and she wanted to stay, on account of close family ties. That incident happened in our store one evening after hours; I witnessed the anguished shouting and crying unnoticed, as I was cowering behind one of the counters. It was a major event, as separation and divorce were virtually unheard of.

The couple came to see my father in hopes of settling their differences. Robert wanted to leave instantly because he believed that Slovakia would be taken over by the Nazis within a few weeks. He was very depressed. He just wanted to go, leaving all possessions behind. He didn't know where to go, he just wanted to get out of Slovakia without delay. At the time, I was happy that Sylvia and their daughter Ruthie stayed behind. I was perhaps swayed by the fact that I thought little Ruthie was by far the most beautiful girl in Trenčín. In the end, Robert could not be deterred and he left Slovakia. Both mother and daughter stayed behind and were killed by the Nazis after the first wave of deportations. I later learned that Robert survived the war and raised a second family in Australia.

In the coming months and years, this was a scene I saw played out many times. Family ties fractured under the strain, and many families were forced to make the choice between the comfort and security of the known and the frightening journey into uncertain fortunes.

Family relationships and behavior were largely dictated by convention and community traditions, but such philosophical guidelines were inadequate to hold families together when the head of the household was forced to confront the wrenching decision of whether to flee, hide, rely on bribes for survival or just fall into line and do what you were told. Decisions were often shaped by the internal strength of families to act with resolution and to take advantage of whatever options remained open to them. Tragically, as time progressed, the options dwindled until finally they disappeared altogether. I think one of the insufficiently explored aspects of the Holocaust concerns how the enormous pain and suffering—both physical and emotional—of life and death in the camps ultimately broke down the conventional rules of family dynamics. In the midst of the madness, husbands abandoned wives, mothers were separated from their children, and grandparents were sacrificed as a way of filling the prescribed quota for the next morning's deportation to the death camps.

Although I did not recognize it at the time, these observations led to my profound belief that one should never allow oneself to be placed in a position where there were no choices for action. For me, personal freedom was defined as the ability to choose from the maximum number of opportunities available in determining how and where to act.

Contemplating Escape

I believe my father was preparing for emigration as early as in 1937. One day I was eating ice cream and Father came into the room and told me to quickly wash my face because someone wanted to take our pictures. It was all very hush-hush and seemed rather odd to me at the time; I later learned that the photographs were for passports. For my father and our family to be seen taking passport pictures would have been a serious mistake, as in those days our friends and neighbors viewed us as exemplars of stability, and this would have set off a panic.

Father also set aside a stockpile of large denomination bank notes, as he knew that if conditions worsened, we could always bribe our way out of the country. Throughout the war, my father continued to be torn about what to do; there were so many competing interests. Should he emigrate and save the family? While I believe this would have been his first choice, he could not. His parents would never agree to move, and he felt a solemn obligation to the many relatives who looked to him for assistance and protection. Ultimately, he chose loyalty to his parents and duty to his extended family before the easier choice of saving himself, his wife, and his children.

As it turned out, my father's efforts to hide away a stash of money were for naught. These emergency funds were given to my mother for safekeeping, as she was the one who minded the family finances and acted as the cashier in the store. She placed the bills in a metal cigar box in the attic where the Passover dishes were stored, sliding it behind a steam radiator for secrecy.

One day my father asked her to retrieve the emergency funds because Andor Kubiček was leaving for the Zionist Congress in Switzerland. While there, Andor was also to set up a Swiss bank account that could be used to finance our family's escape beyond the reach of the Third Reich. As an official delegate, Andor would also be able to obtain the necessary visas and travel tickets in Basel; this was important because any such attempt made in Slovakia would become public. Father was determined to keep all of these preparations secret, in case the situation never became so dire as to warrant execution of the escape plan.

Mother dutifully went up to the attic and fetched down the precious ersatz safe. However, when the stacks of currency were withdrawn from the little metal vault, they just fell to pieces! Apparently, when she had placed the box behind the radiator, it didn't fall all the way down into the space between the floorboards as intended, and the radiator's heat did its worst. The only thing I remember—and I have told my children this story as a way of illustrating what marital bonds and family forgiveness is all about—is that Father didn't utter a word of reproach to my mother, and never mentioned the episode again with this one exception: Years later, the decision Father had made not to escape in 1939 was at least partially justified due to the sudden disappearance of the emergency fund.

Kubiček went to Basel and attempted to make the necessary arrangements for our family as well as his own. When he was unsuccessful, he tried again in Paris, and again he failed. He didn't give up; he again attempt to make the arrangements in Lisbon, before finally departing for the USA in 1942. As a true partner, my father assumed the additional responsibility of caring for and protecting the Kubiček family. Both Mrs. Kubiček and their son survived and emigrated to the United States in 1947.

Fredi Kobler was another member of the Kubiček family who was a good friend of my father. Fredi managed to slip out of Austria just in time to evade Hitler. He went to France and joined the corps being formed by exiled officers from the Czechoslovak Army. As I understand it, Fredi—a magician when it came to adapting to changing circumstances—successfully boarded the last troop transport heading from France to England just as the Wehrmacht was roaring in to close all of the ports. A real wheeler-dealer, Fredi took advantage of every opportunity life afforded him. When he discovered how undervalued real estate was in London, he started investing in hotels and accumulated vast wealth in short order. Throughout my life, I learned to admire Fredi for his tenacity and business acumen; he possessed an instinctive sense about when to cut his losses and when to invest where others were being timid. After the war, Fredi facilitated my escape from soon-to-be Communist Czechoslovakia by registering me as a student in a school for wireless technicians in England. He also helped me get on my feet during my first few years in America. Thanks, Fredi!

The Mindset

To understand what was going on during the years of the gradual tightening of Hitler's stranglehold on European Jewry, it is helpful to enter into the mindset of the Jews in Slovakia. It would seem logical that one would simply want to move beyond the Nazis' clutches. The Zionists wanted to see all Jews emigrate to Palestine, but the idea of becoming an agricultural worker in a communal settlement and being used for target practice by Arabs was not exactly appealing to those outside the Zionist movement. There were, however, other options. While escape was still possible, the list of places to go included such unlikely locales as Cuba, Argentina, Shanghai, Birobidjan (the Jewish state in the Soviet Union), South Africa, Canada, and that most desirable haven for every refugee, the United States of America. So why didn't they all just leave while they could?

The answer is complicated.

The Jews from the farms and villages were the first to be deported to the death camps, as they were easy prey. They were unsophisticated and embraced a parochial view of the world. They had limited resources and an ingrained fear of change—and uprooting the family though emigration certainly constituted change. Further, the very idea of a methodical genocide was simply unimaginable. They found the conceptual model of how to deal with adversity in the Bible: The exodus from Egypt, the Babylonian captivity, the reign of Greek despots, the destruction of the Jewish state by the Romans, and the pogroms in Russia were historical events against which Hitler's threats would be considered. In each case, the lesson of the Bible was that suffering only made the Jews stronger and more resilient.

I must also say that the conservative influence of the local community leaders inhibited a thoughtful and realistic assessment of the Nazi threat. As the unspeakable lethality of the Holocaust emerged gradually, most of the established leadership of the Jewish community continued to tranquilize the population in hopes that somehow they could make a deal with their oppressors. This tendency to compromise and to minimize disruption of traditional folkways finds its fullest manifestation in the deplorable role of the Jewish community leadership in administrative collaboration with the Nazis and their local stooges; in far too many cases, they actually assisted in the mass deportations of Jews to annihilation factories.

There was nothing in the lessons communicated by the rabbis, nothing in the books of the Bible or in the Talmud to prepare the Jewish communities for such a crime against humanity. The rural Jews were simply poor folks eking out a marginal living on their farms or in the villages and small towns, and they couldn't conceive of the monstrous crimes that were being organized and orchestrated with the same cool efficiency that underscored the Germans' industrial prowess. Confronted with a gradually escalating terror, the tendency at every step was either to deny it, minimize it or to choose procrastination as a preferred way of avoiding the obvious.

The Jewish cultural experience over the centuries was always one of enduring persecution, not resisting it—and certainly never taking up arms against their oppressors. It was always considered preferable to disperse, negotiate, emigrate, bribe, accept abject poverty or even bondage until the bad times passed. Fortunes were made, lost and then rebuilt again somewhere else or by different means. Temporary or permanent conversions to Christianity or to the Muslim faith offered escape routes from losses of freedom, livelihood, or accumulated wealth. Such culturally-ingrained experiences were derived from centuries of wandering from one country to another in the wake of expulsions, pogroms, expropriation (which my father initially considered to be the worst-case scenario), lynchings, or mass murder, and they always favored procrastination as the first and most favored option.

That all—or even most—of Trenčín's Jewish community (those who could afford it) would indulge in some biblical reenactment of the exodus was never a practical solution. Except for a few who had connections in distant lands, most of the Jewish community did not have a feeling of urgency to flee when that was still feasible. There was this continual bargaining with a fate that could have perhaps been seen as inevitable if Jewish leadership would have taken a more sober view of what was happening in Germany; there was a clear and well-documented intent to completely destroy European Jewry. I abhor this propensity to look for temporary assurances of safety that relieve us of the will and the responsibility to make hard decisions; one should never accept or associate with anything that is evil, lest they be tainted by it.

The incessant drone of indecision—it can't be that bad; well, maybe I'll do this; maybe I'll compromise on this; maybe it won't be that way; and, I don't know what it will be like when I end up in a strange land—became a form of incremental rationalization that led to collective paralysis when all of the options for escape had vanished. "Incremental rationalization" is a term I coined almost sixty years ago to describe what I have observed in the behavior of Holocaust victims. People, for a number of reasons, were forced to find justification for whatever position they took. All that self-delusion became a one-way ticket to destruction.

For a time escape was possible, but it hinged on perfect timing, risk taking, cold cash, and decisiveness. As I said, there were many places one could emigrate to—I can recall a disreputable Rumanian character who offered us visas to Madagascar (as it turned out, this unlikely angel did in fact manage to save a few souls). There were shady operators hawking Jamaican visas for hard currency; they took a lot of money and then disappeared. The stories about betrayals of desperate refugees are well documented. After all these risks are tallied up and weighed against the mortality statistics associated with the "Final Solution," those who at least made the attempt to get out stood a far better chance of surviving.

Ironically, the risks involved in emigrating turned out to be far lower than the risks that fell to those who chose to remain and take their chances with the Nazis. My personal risk calculator continued to function at a high level, even after my arrival in what is still the safest place on earth, the USA. I exercised it during the Cuban Missile Crisis when I removed my family to our summer cottage in Duchess County. I selected the location because it was in a vale surrounded by hills that blocked the path of fallout in the event of a nuclear strike on New York. When traveling by air, I habitually select seats next to an emergency exit. And to this day I serve as the Emergency Preparedness merit badge counselor for my local scout troop and advocate for greater emergency funding as a member of my neighborhood Emergency Preparedness Operations Center. I am a life member of the National Rifle Association and I firmly believe in the right to keep and bear arms. All my boys have been well trained in the use of firearms for self-defense and two are qualified sharpshooters.

Part III

Slovakia

THE NOOSE

On the first of September, 1939, German and Slovakian troops invaded Poland, thus marking the outbreak of World War II. My scout troop was camping near Levoča, in the Tatra Mountains near the Polish border. The booming sounds of exploding bombs and shells echoed across the mountains to the north of us early in the morning hours and woke us with a start.

After raising the flag, our troop leader, Akiba Neufeld, informed us that war had broken out; we had to pack up instantly and head for home. We stowed our gear hastily and departed by train, singing on the way, as only innocent young men do in the face of war. We actually welcomed the coming war as a solution to all our troubles.

For the next few days, life continued as always, but Father's anxieties were plainly visible. My usually calm mother, too, was very perturbed. Nobody knew what would happen next. With Britain's declaration of war followed almost immediately by that of France, a number of optimists spread jubilant rumors that after a brief spate of battles, the Germans would surely be defeated.

The Path to War

Following the abandonment of Czechoslovakia by the French and British in the Munich Pact of September, 1938, the Wehrmacht occupied the Sudetenland (the borderland of what is now the Czech Republic) without resistance. Czechoslovakia was forced to evacuate its border fortifications and the country became effectively defenseless. This diplomatic ploy—a policy known as "appeasement"—emboldened Hitler to declare that he would destroy Czechoslovakia by occupying it later, and so he did.

Beginning in 1938, it was obvious that the Slovaks would collaborate with the Germans to bring Czechoslovakia under the control of the German Reich. The dominant Slovak political parties announced full support of Hitler's expansionary plans. Slovakia had been under the Hungarian boot for centuries and banked on a deal with the Germans as the road to an independent state. Slovak leaders hitched their dreams to the Nazis' star—after all, it appeared to be rising, so why not throw in with what looked like the winning side? Independence would also mean a split with the Czechs, who were a more cosmopolitan, protestant, and formerly Austrian culture.

The separatist moves toward Slovak independence generated a glimmer of hope among the Jews that perhaps they would be spared the indignities that Czech Jews were sure to suffer once they came under German control. As a client state of the Reich, it was hoped that Slovakia would not be occupied by the German Army, and its population would not be subjected to the increasingly restrictive Nazi laws. It was further assumed that Germany would not much care about controlling Slovakia, for unlike the Czech regions, Slovakia did not offer the lure of a well-developed armaments industry. Such speculation bolstered the rationalization that doing nothing would be the most prudent position for Slovak Jews to take.

Indeed, the Germans did not occupy Slovakia, because they were concentrating on preparations to wage war on France and England. Meanwhile, life in Trenčín continued without much disruption. Only the most farsighted Jews left without delay to whatever country would accept them. The exodus to Palestine was also accelerated, but that was seen as an option mostly for the young Zionists who had been training for hardships and physical labor. Most of the Jews who lived in Slovakian towns and cities were merchants, small business owners, professionals, and tradespeople who were used to a relatively high quality of life. There were also elderly people, families with small children, and owners of property who just couldn't visualize picking up and going to a strange place where they would have to start from the bottom rung of the economic ladder, in lands where speaking in a foreign tongue would be obligatory.

The Jews who left first were wealthy lawyers. I remember two families who had cultivated connections with families abroad. One was a Trenčín lawyer named Ringwald who began to unload his sizeable real estate holdings in 1936. When the Slovak Republic was established, Ringwald was already comfortably resettled in England. The Petscheks from Prague were prominent bankers with well-established international connections. Their children had been educated in fine English schools. When invasion became imminent, they got out. Families who had established links with relatives abroad (a centuries-old Jewish survival skill) and had the foresight to deposit money in foreign banks found it relatively easy to obtain visas and depart with little fanfare.

Meanwhile, my father's business affairs went ahead apace. But while everything looked normal on the surface, my father was making arrangements for a trusted associate to take over the business if it was threatened with confiscation. At this early stage, the worst-case scenario among the remaining Jews was the anticipation of loss of property. Efforts were therefore focused on finding ways for assets to be transferred to gentiles with whom they had a trusted relationship.

In our case, my father started strengthening his relationship with Jan Bonko, a prominent member of the Slovak right wing and a leader of the local Hlinka Party who was also associated with the Catholic Church. Bonko was a small shopkeeper who had been a client of our wholesale firm for many years. He also had an ambitious wife who was very eager to take possession of the Strassmann properties.

The expropriation of Jewish property (Aryanization, or *Arisierung*) began around the end of 1939. The name Strassmann was removed from the marquee on top of our store to be replaced by Bonko & Strassmann. Not surprisingly, Mrs. Bonko took over the cash register. My father became an underpaid bookkeeper in his own business; his experience was essential to keep the enterprise operating efficiently. Meanwhile, we were forced to vacate our living quarters so that the Bonko family could move in. Shortly thereafter Bonko took over the entire business under the singular firm name of "Jan Bonko." His family now occupied the entire commercial complex my father had built in 1934.

The Legal Phase

The proclamation of the Slovak Republic in March of 1939 marked the decisive step in shaping the future of Slovak Jews. Jozef Tiso became the prime minister of this Nazi puppet regime. The Hlinka People's Party was the only party that was legally allowed to function—it was in essence a dictatorship. Slovakia became an ally of Germany and provided rail and road access for transporting Wehrmacht troops and materiel. During the Nazi invasion of Poland, and later on the Eastern Front, Slovakia was also called on to provide fighting troops. In October of 1939, Tiso was elected president, pro-Nazi Voytech Tuka replaced him as prime minister and the rabid anti-Semite, Šano Mach, was named minister of the interior and assumed control of the Hlinka Guard. This fascistic team set out to build the machinery for the subjugation and, in due course, elimination of the Jews.

To gain legitimacy in expanding Hitler's empire, the Slovak government pledged that their new state would adopt the Nuremberg Laws that escalated the restrictions placed on Jewish life. In April 1939, the new Slovak state enacted anti-Jewish legislation by an overwhelming parliamentary majority, defining the status of Jews along religious rather than racial lines. This distinction was a departure from the usual approach the Nazis applied to every other European country that came under German control. This reflected the fact that Slovakia was a staunchly Catholic country, ruled by a priest who saw all distinctions among people in theological terms. It is now suggested that reports of the mass murder of Slovak Jews in death camps in Poland were provided to the Tiso government by the Papal Nuncio in Bratislava, resulting in the cessation of the deportation of Jews in the fall of 1942.

In many respects, the Slovak approach to the resolution of what came to be called the "Jewish Question" was seen initially as less inhumane than the practices followed by the Nazis in other lands. Consequently Jews rationalized their circumstances by simply accepting what they could not change; the only way to survive was to comply with the new Slovak regulations.

SS *Haupsturmfuhrer* Dieter Wisliceny, Adolf Eichmann's representative from the Reich Security Main Office, arrived in Bratislava as an adviser on Jewish affairs in August 1940. The Hlinka Guard and the *Freiwillige Schutzstaffel* (Slovak volunteers in the SS) were then reorganized and given responsibility for implementing anti-Jewish measures. The sequence of how such measures were to be implemented was dictated by a careful legal progression calculated to strip the Jews of all their property. This required minimal effort, while rewarding the loyal backers of the new order with the spoils without creating internal dissent.

On September 9, 1941, the Slovak government promulgated an elaborate body of anti-Jewish legislation and regulations. It contained 270 articles, which included requiring Jews to wear the identifying yellow Star of David, rendering them subject to forced labor without pay and evicting them from specified towns as well as from specifically designated streets and houses (listed by house number). It put a legal face on "ethnic cleansing."

As long as it was Slovaks who were implementing these Nazi rules, one could always hope to be dealing with people they knew and understood. Under such circumstances the age-tested patterns of Jewish survival—negotiation for some sort of accommodation—could at least be tried. Unfortunately, those old ways no longer worked. The machinery that still reflected habits remaining from the days of the Austro-Hungarian Empire led the Jews into submission and ultimately, death.

The Stranglehold

The restrictions began in late 1939. The bureaucratic thoroughness by which laws and regulations were deployed for the progressive degradation of the Jews is uniquely revealed through a collection of papers I donated to the United States Holocaust Memorial Museum in Washington, DC. The archive comprises over fifty certificates and receipts documenting the sequential destruction of the life of an innkeeper from a village near Trenčín.

The papers had been preserved in a shoebox which was salvaged by a friend of my sister's. She gave the container and its contents to my sister, and Ella then passed these precious historical artifacts on to me. They are evidence; they clearly outline the successive steps taken by Slovak authorities to eliminate the Jews. The methods were borrowed from the Nazis, and while they were not as brutally enforced, they were just as efficient at using legal sleight of hand to prosecute the economic strangulation of the Slovak Jews. One by one, laws were passed to strip the Jews of their property, their rights, their dignity, their humanity, and ultimately their lives. In each instance, these statutes and ordinances were approved by the unanimous vote of representatives elected by popular vote.

The innkeeper in question was a World War I veteran; he was an invalid who had received a coveted liquor license as a privilege that was granted to wounded war veterans. The shoebox contained a rumpled copy of an elaborate legal measure stating that Jews did not qualify to function as innkeepers. Within sixty days of this declaration, every Jewish innkeeper had to surrender his license, which was in turn handed over to a designated supporter of the Slovak state. The only qualification for the new innkeeper was an endorsement by the local Hlinka Guards unit, the self-appointed paramilitary guardians of the state.

This legal thievery continued in the postwar years, when claims by Jews for restitution were rejected on the grounds that such expropriations were conducted under the laws then on the books, laws that were passed by the parliamentary processes of a sovereign state. Hence there were no "crimes" committed against the Jews, and without a crime, there was no victim, without a victim, no restitution. All very neat and orderly.

The custom of legal expropriation has a long history in Eastern Europe, where frequent regime changes invariably displaced property holders, replacing them with those in political favor. Violent turnovers were often accompanied by local uprisings, undertaken to evict holders of old privileges and mask the wholesale looting that followed. To the non-Jewish population, the eviction of the Slovak Jews was just another historical turn, a vaguely legitimate opportunity to acquire assets with a minimum of effort.

The quasi-legal appropriation of property from those who lost the protection of the state was continued by the Communists with a zeal that exceeded even that of the Nazis. It must be difficult for the younger readers of these pages—especially if they are American—to comprehend the circumstances I witnessed after the end of the war. Whenever I walked down a street in Slovakia, I could see evidence of government-sponsored theft.

Legalization of Theft

Once the Jewish innkeepers' livelihood had been stripped away, the question remained: What to do with them? This was a dilemma that I experienced personally, as two of my uncles had been innkeepers and were suddenly destitute. Of course, they had to rely on the charity of their extended families. As the war continued with unabated German victories, the Nazi methods of dealing with the "Jewish Question" called for the isolation of Jews from the rest of the population. For their part, the Slovak authorities passed another regulation prohibiting Jews from possessing radios with shortwave frequency capability. Shortly thereafter, all radios were banned. Then, you could not have a telephone or a vacuum cleaner or a camera.

If you had a radio, or any item on the prohibited list, you had to hand it over to the local police who then issued you an official-looking receipt. The police then proceeded to distribute the radios to the Hlinka party faithful who were now charged with the added responsibility of performing house-checks, to ensure that the Jews were complying with the rising number of restrictions. Although this process was aimed at subjugating the Jews, it also served as a means for the party loyalists to impose control over the orderly distribution of loot to select recipients. This policy also drew more citizens into participation in state-sanctioned robbery.

By the spring of 1940, the sequential collection of the receipts in the shoebox began to increase. The burden was shifted onto the Jews to show compliance with restrictions and to be able to prove that nothing remained hidden. The steady stream of restrictive individual laws and administrative regulations were now gathered together in a detailed set of codes. Any violation was used as a pretext for imposing additional penalties. For example, in a detailed proclamation appearing in the daily press the state decreed certain items of clothing that were henceforth prohibited, as well as identifying specific apartments that would have to be given up. Those seeking possession of choice living quarters gladly assisted in the compilation of the lists. In a number of cases, additional locations were added as a special favor to loyal citizens. Jews were summarily evicted from their houses on short notice—even furniture had to be left behind for the new occupants. If you lived in a house above a store on a street where business was conducted you had to hand over your keys to a preselected party functionary. The evicted families were essentially concentrated into ghettos. The innkeeper whose life was documented in the shoebox was forced to take up residence in the back of a farmer's barn with only the barest essentials.

The innkeeper's document collection continued to grow rapidly. There were bogus "receipts" for cameras, fur coats, jackets with fur collars, valuables (such as jewelry), certificates of declaration regarding bank accounts, proof that no debts were owed, a receipt for the payment of "transportation costs" to send his only son to a labor camp in Poland, and finally the stark, ghoulish notice to report in the morning to the local railroad station for "transfer to an unspecified location." Unbelievably, the innkeeper and his wife were required to provide prepayment of a "transportation fee" of 500 Reichmarks each to be sent to their deaths. That was an enormous sum in 1940, a final insult to the Jews being deported. Not that it mattered much; they wouldn't be needing money where they were going.

All of the receipts for property and persons received official-looking stamps and were recorded on mimeographed forms. These were usually headed by the phrase "According to Paragraph XX, the undersigned acknowledges receipt for YY." All of this was done to preserve the appearance that a perfectly legal business transaction was taking place.

Jews as Property

The fares thus collected to transport victims crammed into cattle cars cheek-by-jowl were dutifully handed over by the Slovak authorities to turn over this money Eichmann's SS for the operation of the death camps. Slovak law defined such transfers as "exchanges of property," thereby absolving the Slovak functionaries of all responsibility for their citizens. By depriving Jews of all civil rights and reducing them to the state of "property," the Nazis and their Slovak collaborators were invoking the ancient Roman doctrine governing the conduct of the slave trade.

Slovakia bears the dubious distinction of being the only country in Europe that paid the Nazis for the deportation of its Jews. It was a shoddy trick to provide moral justification for heinous crimes against humanity. The Slovak authorities knew the fate of the Jews they were deporting, but this carefully rigged subterfuge allowed them to feign ignorance.

I remember how the Slovak press featured numerous stories showing pictures of well-fed Slovak Jews in very presentable factories merrily sewing uniforms for the Wehrmacht and thus contributing to the Nazi war effort. Such propaganda was employed to tranquilize whatever scrap of conscience remained in the non-Jewish Slovak population. These carefully crafted stories were also intended to convince the Jews that life in a labor camp might not be so bad, and that they would surely survive the war by simply keeping quiet and doing what they were told.

These carefully kept accounts—the bills of lading for the human cargo that the Slovak authorities were shipping to Poland for the SS—were damning physical evidence of routinized, government-sanctioned genocide. The existence of such incontrovertible evidence may have begun to haunt a few Slovaks, particularly the Catholic clergy. By the summer of 1942, more than 80 percent of the Jewish population of Slovakia had been shipped off to death camps in Poland and someone very high up in the hierarchy of the church must have become apprehensive. What would the world say, what would the retribution be, if the Germans lost the war? I am now convinced that it is no coincidence that the interdiction of the Catholic Church in the deportation of the Jews happened to coincide with the news that the vaunted Wehrmacht was suffering defeat after defeat on the battlefield.

Family Deprivations

The next shock received by my family occurred in early 1941, when we were ordered to vacate the two back rooms of our well-appointed six-room residence and take up residence in a small two-room apartment near the Lutheran church. Father secured these quarters when he discovered that that address had somehow been omitted from the prohibited list. So we left the house and business my Father had built, leaving most of the custom furniture in place for the Bonkos.

Ella and I slept in the living room. Our parents occupied the bedroom, which also doubled as the storage room and pantry. Considering the circumstances, the living conditions in the new place were not bad. Father arranged for the move to be done as smoothly as possible.

I think the whole thing was tolerable because no one could have guessed the fate that was awaiting us. The general sentiment in those days was one of optimistic resignation: "The war is here, but the war will pass, and somehow we'll survive"; "Jews have survived adversity before"; and, "How bad can it get?"

The borders had been closed since mid-1939. Jews could not get passports. One could only leave illegally, and even that was contingent upon obtaining a counterfeit visa from a country that would accept a Jew. There weren't many. Our window of escape had closed firmly shut; it was impossible for our family to contemplate evasion of the authorities with our retinue of grandparents, dependent relatives, and children. The Jews were now stuck in Slovakia, physically as well as psychologically. The only alternative was to learn how to submit to the new regime while suffering the least amount of pain and indignity. That meant applying the lessons learned by Jews over the centuries.

The only glimmers from the rapidly closing outside world were occasional messages smuggled in by the most devious methods imaginable. I vaguely recall an attempt to help Fredi Kobler's mother escape from the Nazi grip by moving to San Remo, Italy, in 1940. Apparently, treaties dating back to the fourteenth century empowered San Remo to act as a sovereign state in some cases. I only mention this incident to show that the Nazi net had holes, which could be exploited if audacity and money were liberally applied. A few of the more venturesome actually managed to get out through Rumania, traveling through Turkey and on to Palestine.

Sixty years on, it is difficult for me to explain my feelings and reactions to my rapidly-changing surroundings. I was young and innocent; I could only sense my parents' growing anxiety and an increased sense of isolation from the community. My parents did their best to shield my sister and me from the truth, keeping quiet about their own troubles and resorting to conversing in Hungarian whenever confidences had to be exchanged. We had no idea what they might (or might not) be planning.

Plunder

From snippets of conversation I overheard between my parents I discerned that many of our household belongings were being gradually disposed of as "gifts"—which is to say, bribes. There was much discussion about whether we should leave our lovely Persian rugs for the Bonkos or use them to grease the administrative wheels as we navigated the treacherous waters of political patronage. I also remember the debate about what to do with our expensive Contax camera; ultimately, it was given away as appreciation for some unspecified accommodation. We started shedding things voluntarily because they were going to be seized anyway, so we now might as well derive some small advantage from the process.

After the liberation, we were unable to reclaim most of our property, as the new owners generally claimed these objects were legitimate gifts received in return for some consideration or other. Such bald-faced thievery from one's own neighbors poisoned me against remaining in Slovakia. With the coming threat of a Communist takeover, I anticipated a repeat performance of the long history of plundering and repression whenever a new political regime was installed.

Even today, much of the accumulated wealth in Slovakia can be traced to expropriations of Hungarian landowners after the end of World War I, to the seizing of property from the Czechs in 1939, followed by the same governmentally-sanctioned thievery from the Jews in 1940–42, to the reclamation of stolen property from the Germans in 1945, to the "nationalization" of the capitalists' property in 1948, and finally, to the large-scale pilfering of state property in the wake of the demise of the Communist regime in 1998. Everyone seems bent on stealing the defeated enemy's ill-gotten gains.

The dark story of politically sanctioned injustice in Slovakia has a long pedigree. It has made a lasting imprint on the behavior of the inhabitants of that part of the world. Habits that favor oppression, plunder, theft, and corruption will not be expunged for generations to come.

The conduct of the population has been influenced by its cynical understanding that it was advantageous to support the legitimacy of looting by means of fancy legal footwork. That is why my father was burdened with a flood of declarations and affidavits to account for all of his property and all of his financial relationships from 1939 through 1941. As time went on, it became obvious that it was the Nazis' intent to systematically strip the Jews of their civil liberties and self-respect, then their property and livelihoods, and finally their very existence.

State-organized plunder can be very useful in assuring loyalty, creating a cadre of dedicated henchmen willing to perform unspeakable acts, and padding the state coffers without taxing the citizenry. When the fascist Slovak Republic functionaries were deciding that Jews may not reside on a particular street, or not own such-and-such possessions, regulations were drafted with the full cooperation of party faithful, who were already dividing up the spoils. That's why the Jewish experience in Slovakia didn't involve the brutal nighttime roundups of entire communities that characterized the Nazi's ethnic cleansing program elsewhere in Central and Eastern Europe. On one level, the gradual destruction of the Jewish community in Slovakia was just a cleverly conceived and self-financing business venture.

The methodical theft of Jewish property was conducted from June 1939 to March of 1942. When the Jews were finally reduced to abject poverty, emotional despondency and humiliation, they were ready for shipment to the death camps—with their spirit broken, they wouldn't put up a fight. This process appeared to be the orderly eviction of unwanted tenants, rather than the corralling of a herd headed for the slaughterhouse.

For a while the Jews were fooled into believing that what was happening was merely a more extreme replay of an age-old phenomenon that was uncomfortable, but survivable.

What made the Jewish holocaust in Slovakia historically unprecedented was its scope. Consider that something on the order of 15 percent of all real property in Slovakia had been confiscated. The Slovak holocaust was also more lethal than the genocide in other areas: A mind-boggling

93 percent of the Jewish population was ultimately murdered. The Slovak authorities were more devious than the Germans; their implementation of legal devices designed to accomplish the hideous deed while leaving their consciences clear was both incredibly efficient and highly successful. It was cold-blooded, bureaucratically-sanctioned murder.

The Business of Mass Murder

The Nazi form of genocide is unique in the annals of history—different from the mass slaying of the Armenians, Native Americans, Tutsi tribesmen, Kosovars, and Cambodians. For the Nazis, extermination was a well-conceived, systematic process optimized to execute racist laws with an accountant's eye toward efficiency. Although well over a hundred million people have been killed in genocidal acts since the end of World War II, with the exception of the mass executions of the Stalinist regime, only the Nazi method could be categorized as industrialized genocide. The leaders were not homicidal maniacs like Charles Manson; rather, they were reasonably well-educated, businesslike engineers of death. Indeed, they felt morally justified in committing their atrocities.

The Slovak version of genocide imitated the German model in that it took special pains to make sure that all actions taken against the Jews were procedurally correct. A number of Western governments have recognized the racially-motivated legislation enacted by the fascist Slovak Republic as being laws that were passed by a duly-elected legislature, following a meticulous and well-documented judicial process. The system was rigged to eliminate the possibility of any appeals. Consequently, the Slovak genocide was only rarely accompanied by overt acts of violence against unarmed civilians (as was customary whenever SS troops took control of a particular region). In Slovakia the Jews marched meekly to their destruction in an orderly process that was administered by their own community leaders.

Machinery of Genocide

My firsthand experiences with the "Final Solution" have sharpened my comprehension of how a totalitarian state can destroy any population it chooses while the world looks on and does nothing to prevent it. This experience also galvanized my outlook on politics, and on the actions a civilized society must take to safeguard the rights of individuals. My views of the dynamics of the Holocaust differ from much of the accepted lore. A great deal of Holocaust historiography recounts the record of brutal beatings, indescribable suffering, and wholesale murder. Those stories are all true and well documented. But insufficient attention has been devoted to the processes that facilitated those atrocities. The organization of the machinery of extermination in the Nazi-supported police states in France, Belgium, Holland, Hungary, Austria, Greece, Croatia, and Italy offer grim case studies in how easy it is for a dominant military power to subvert law and justice.

With the passage of time, it becomes increasingly difficult to comprehend how the Nazis managed to implement the Holocaust in broad daylight, right under the world's nose. It is critical that succeeding generations, weaned on personal freedom and a sense of entitlement, understand how every modern state—and particularly a police state—that acquires the computerized capacity to monitor its citizens' actions, has the ability to pervert its institutions and use them as instruments of slavery or genocide. The means exist for the Nazi nightmare to occur again.

The "wild" idea that a government could leverage information technologies (rather than brute force) to effect the complete control and subjugation of its citizenry became a popular topic with the 1949 publication of George Orwell's dystopian social science fiction thriller, *Nineteen Eighty-Four*. Orwell described a society in which a dictatorial power (Big Brother) employed transceiving television cameras to spy on everyone at all times. From a technical perspective, I found a visually-monitored police state economically and operationally unfeasible. Calculating the percentage of the population that would have to be employed in keeping track of every corner of every room as well as of every vehicle at all times, without errors yields an unrealistic number of human monitors. The cost of setting up an auditing system to assure perfect compliance, as well as the expense of constantly videotaping everything would be economically crippling. Indexing, storage, and context-based retrieval of such a huge volume of videotaped evidence cannot be performed, even with today's advanced supercomputers.

It happened that while I was speculating about Orwell's vision of the future, an international group of independent scholars convened a three-day conference in Geneva in 1983 to explore "Orwellian threats" to society. Harlan Cleveland, the former US under-secretary of state and a great humanist, headed the consortium. As an experienced computer programmer, I delivered a paper that offered a detailed account of how a police state could use computerized networks to control the media, education, and consumer spending habits, as well as to track the movements of anyone it desired. As an executive at Xerox, I had already witnessed the potential of the Advanced Research Project Agency Networks (ARPANET, precursor of the internet) to deliver an Orwellian society at a low cost. The meeting participants, many of them from underdeveloped countries, found my techno-thriller scenario implausible. Yet much of what I hypothesized then has come to pass. One of these days, I will publish an updated version of my Geneva paper and demonstrate how much "progress" we have made in our efforts to acquire the technological capability to control the freedoms of a civil society—without resorting to the use of violence.

Everyday Life

The Jewish school in Trenčín was closed in 1940 or early '41. My father retained private tutors to continue my studies (and keep me out of mischief). These sidelined professors were always looking for tutoring jobs, even for the few pennies my father could offer. I particularly remember Professor Vikar, a demanding instructor of mathematics and physics. Vikar tasked me with keeping the physics instruments in his laboratory in working condition. Professor Kumprecht taught chemistry and geography. I also started learning English with Lucy Muller, a refugee from Austria, and continued my piano lessons with Mrs. Dubnicay, the hypersensitive wife of a district criminal judge. Father really could not afford such a luxury, but I guess that teaching the son of a leading citizen was viewed more as an act of charity than business.

In the Jewish school, the students were crowded into three classes covering ages six to fifteen. In 1942, my class had an age range from nine to fifteen. It also included children with all sorts of disabilities. Time was wasted and the lessons were utterly boring because we all had to sit still and listen to uninteresting lectures that catered to the slowest learners. There were very few textbooks and most of the tutorial material was gained from what was written on the blackboard with chalk.

During the tutoring period, I developed study habits that served me well in the years to come. Because time was at a premium, the tutorial sessions were always organized for maximum progress. I had to study harder and with greater attention than ever before. These conditions forced me to acquire a lifelong habit of relying on independent learning from books instead of listening to lectures.

The Yellow Star

I started wearing the yellow star in 1942. This method of segregating the Jews and drawing attention to them would, along with the registry logs, become the precursor for the deportations to Poland. The enforcement of the yellow star policy made it easy for the Hlinka Guards to round up people specified on a deportation list.

There was a limited supply of yellow stars because they had to be securely sewn onto individual garments. The stars were made in Jewish workshops and were distributed through the local Jewish community. How and where to place the yellow star was a topic of much discussion, even though the regulations were quite explicit. Which jacket were you to put it on if you had more than one? Where were you to place it if you had a wide collar that would partially cover the star? My paternal grandmother would not accept the yellow mark of indignity. A diminutive lady, she had a large pocketbook that could be carried in an unassuming manner that completely covered up the hated star. She was elderly and nobody ever bothered her, although after the wearing of the star started to be enforced more zealously she hardly ever ventured out on the streets.

Wearing the yellow star in a small town (where most people knew each other) became an unceasing source of embarrassment. That was precisely the effect that the Hlinka Guard intended to create; the star represented the ultimate public humiliation. Having no radio, no books, no movies, no music, no furs, no privileges to attend any entertainment or restaurants while being limited to only prescribed places during appointed hours were all degradations that could be borne stoically. Wearing a yellow star was an invitation to mugging by the local hooligans who made a sport of harassing Jews. And we didn't dare strike back.

DEPORTATIONS

The deportations began in the spring of 1942. The deportation lists were compiled by the local *Judensraat* (Jewish Community Council) based on a specified quota. The list was then handed over to the local Hlinka Guard command, which operated under the watchful eye of two or three Gestapo officers who were generally Slovaks of German origin. The entire process was driven by the railroad schedules; it was all very businesslike. The deportation quota set for the Trenčín district was calculated based on the carrying capacity of the freight cars and the number of cars available. For maximum efficiency, this often called for jamming as many as eighty people in a single freight car.

As I recall, able-bodied young men were deported first under the guise of needing labor to support the war effort. I think it is more likely that the real purpose was to get rid of potential troublemakers, those who were most likely to resist. Next came the young women. They were deported for the ostensible purpose of sewing winter uniforms for the troops on the Eastern Front.

It was an exceedingly efficient operation carried out with a minimum of fuss. Only a handful of Germans were needed to hand over orders to the local black shirts who in turn passed the quota on to the Judensraat. Copies were also provided to the local police and sometimes also to the gendarmes (paramilitary law enforcement officers). This redundancy was intentional: The police were not averse to accepting a "financial consideration" to remove a name from the list, but the gendarmes were not so corruptible. Further, since the police was a municipal institution comprised largely career civil servants, the officers were well integrated into the community. They could bend some of the rules for Jews they knew personally. The gendarmes was the enforcement arm of the state and was thus better armed (since its primary purpose was to maintain civil order). The gendarmes answered to the central government, and did what it was ordered to do.

Local policemen handled the logistics—rounding up the unfortunates and loading them onto the freight cars. This maintained a sense of propriety and insured compliance. The Hlinka Guard usually hovered on the fringes, ready to apply force if necessary. They need not have worried; the Jews of Trenčín went quietly to their deaths.

What little brutality was dispensed was usually at the hands of the lower ranking members of the Hlinka Guard. These men were uneducated opportunists leveraging the fascist regime as a means of upgrading their social and economic status. Their primary objective was to make sure that the Jewish property was seized and properly recorded. This was the means by which the Hlinka Party acquired wealth for distribution to its supporters.

At the entrance to Trenčín's main square, a former Jewish clothing store had been converted into a pawnshop where items that had been removed from abandoned Jewish homes were laid out on tables to be haggled over on the days immediately following a deportation. Of course, the more valuable items were long gone. Peasants from neighboring villages attending the Sunday market day after mass used the proceeds from the sale of their farm products to load their carts with Jewish goods.

Poor Jews were likely to be deported before the more well to do, to allow more time to shake down the desperate professionals, merchants, and businessmen. Similarly, Jews living in the villages were deported before the city-dwellers. The more cosmopolitan Jews in the cities had more property to loot, and clearing out the villages eliminated potential hiding places.

The methodical nature of this ethnic cleansing operation was facilitated by meticulously recorded census data showing age, occupation, and religion, as well as real estate assets. This demographic data was further refined after 1940 by elaborate surveys of Jews to include information such as savings accounts, currency holdings, insurance policies, and itemization of all valuables (including carpets, fur coats, cameras, and china). They required declarations about any foreign relations, by age, city, and location. Any errors or omissions in filling out these forms were liable to criminal penalties and fines.

When the Jewish community administrators were given a deportation order, the bidding started by first offering a list of names that would fill the scheduled transportation capacity according to the requisition while still leaving room for some exceptions. Within minutes after a deportation order was handed over to a Jewish official (usually two days prior to the arrival of the freight cars), the negotiations began—desperate people frantically seeking a loophole that would disqualify a loved one. Since the required deportee quotas had to be met, the days leading up to the publication of the revised (and final) deportation list were accompanied by heartrending episodes. The emotional relief of learning that a family was not on tomorrow's list was tempered by the realization that this was only a deferral, not a release.

In that horrific spring and summer of 1942, no one knew that after 60,000 of the 80,000 Slovak Jews had been shipped off to the extermination camps, the trains of death would suddenly stop rolling. The reasons for this abrupt cessation are debated to this day.

My sister owes her life to my father's ingenuity. It was early 1942 when the deportations were gearing up and as a hale and hearty teenager Ella was prime material for relocation to a "reeducation" camp. My father did not believe that story and saw to it that her arm was placed in a convincing plaster cast. This disqualified her as an able-bodied worker. As soon as the last transport departed, the cumbersome cast was removed. Much of the musculature in her arm atrophied and she never fully recovered from that disability, but she is alive today.

Holocaust Informatics

One of the contributions I made to the U.S. Holocaust Memorial Museum in Washington, D.C., was to demonstrate the role of punch-card accounting machines as used by the Nazis to efficiently schedule the rail transportation of Jews to the death camps. Although the railroad infrastructure in Eastern Europe was overloaded by military demands, the transportation of Jews to the camps was always given priority. Through my connections at the British Museum of Technology, I tracked down a rare IBM machine manufactured in 1932 by the Deutsche Hollerith Gesellschaft (DEHOMAG) company, an IBM subsidiary since the late 1920s. Still operating in Dresden in 1998, it was identical to the machines originally housed at the Matthausen camp that were used for scheduling the deportation trains to the death camps.

The Holocaust Museum purchased the machine and stored it in a warehouse near Baltimore, where I authenticated it. A fellow IBM executive (now retired) confirmed the support provided by DEHOMAG to the Nazi regime and provided me with the requisite technical documentation for the machine. The circumstantial culpability of the IBM Corporation in this lurid business is addressed in *IBM and the Holocaust* (a book for which I provided technical consultation).[8]

There is no "smoking gun" proof that IBM personnel played an active role in scheduling deportations or knew what the machines were being used for. I find this to be specious; I was responsible for managing an IBM tabulating installation from 1956 through 1959, and the claim that IBM systems engineers were kept away from what was then a sophisticated machine accounting application is not credible. Alleging that the IBM experts did not know what kinds of data were being run at a major tabulating installation—and an SS facility specializing in concentration camp management—beggars belief.

In 1990, I started working with a distinguished author and Holocaust historian, Dr. Sybil Milton, on an exhibit panel to accompany the display of the IBM tabulating equipment at the museum. The display was designed to demonstrate the "bureaucratization of the Holocaust." While it documented a historical fact, it also served as a cautionary tale: Any dictator can harness information technology to repeat such horrors. I regret that the museum elected to allocate only minimal space to this theme. The pain, anguish and ghastly horrors of the atrocities perpetrated by the Nazis now occupies almost all of the exhibit space.

It is also distressing to me to see that the US Holocaust Memorial Museum showed very little interest in addressing the role of Jewish anti-

[8]Black, E., *IBM and the Holocaust*, Crown Publishers, New York, 2001.

Nazi resistance. The only way in which I can explain such a myopic view is by understanding the persistent inclination of most Jews to cast themselves as helpless victims of acts committed by zealous anti-Semites. Personally, I tend to temper this view by seeing the Holocaust also as a deliberate act of genocide. Such tendencies can be diagnosed in advance by listening to the rhetoric of emerging tyrants. In a number of cases—be it Leningrad in 1919, Munich in 1928, Sarajevo in 1990, or Kampala in 1995—the approaching genocide should have been anticipated and countered by timely intervention before the killing began.

Holocaust Disinformation

The placid submission of the Slovak Jews being led to their deaths can also be explained by the skillful manipulation of information by the sophisticated murderers. The German and Slovak intentions were to cover up their crimes against humanity. Simultaneously, the information conveyed by the Jewish leadership reflected the wishful thinking that the horrors awaiting the deported families would somehow be bearable. Over the years I discovered that those who are powerless especially dislike the bearers of bad news. The Jewish leadership feared that publicizing what they knew about the situation in Poland could only lead to resistance and the inevitable violent reprisals. Their choice: say nothing, maintain calm and order. Thus, they inadvertently assisted the Nazis in carrying out their program of genocide.

As Jewish families were loaded into freight cars, those who remained behind pleaded for letters to be written upon safe arrival. The most frequent tranquilizer (and the message widely accepted by the Slovak citizenry and press) was the assertion that the entire relocation of the population was for the purpose of supplying "useful" work[9] in support of the German war effort. The Slovak press delighted in perpetuating the charade about the well being of the deported Jews. Receipts for food parcels were received without much delay, bolstering the stories about good

[9]Those entering the extermination camp at Auschwitz II (Birkenau) passed through gates crowned by the inspiring epithet, *Arbeit macht frei*—Work will set you free.

living conditions. None of these pretenses about the alleged living conditions in Poland could be verified, because there were no independent sources of news.

The transport of Jews to extermination camps in Poland was further complicated by the decision of corrupt Slovak officials to create their own slave labor camps in Slovakia. Because the treatment of Jews in these more local camps could not be as readily obscured, inmates received relatively benign treatment, thus masking the brutality and lethality of conditions in Poland. The reason for keeping a small number of Jews in Slovakia (never more than 5,000 or 6,000 at a time) was to exploit their skills in carpentry and in metal trades. With cooperation from the remaining Jewish community, the deportations to the Slovak labor camps were always seen as the preferred option for anyone who could be classified as an able-bodied craftsman. Such slave labor camps were established in Nováky, Vyhne, Sered, Žilina, Nitra, Láb, and Zohor. Conditions were survivable, though the inmates were occasionally subjected to physical abuse. This was particularly true from 1941 to 1943—that is, while the Germans were winning the war. The abuses diminished following the German retreat from Stalingrad. Camp guards became more circumspect and began to hedge their bets.

The inmates lived in flimsy barracks, suffered from cold in winter, did not have enough food, and received only barely minimal medical care. As the transports to Poland were getting filled up much of the pleading and bargaining over whom to save concentrated on questions of who would be transported to one of the Slovak camps. Nováky had the "best" reputation because its post office functioned and it was relatively better managed as a self-organized community than the other locations.

The "White Card" Exemption

As the deportations proceeded, inexorably depleting the Jewish population in train-size increments, it became obvious to my father that the journey to Poland was a one-way trip. Whether my father actually knew about what was going on at Auschwitz was never clear to me. The stories were so horrific that their message was inconceivable. Such news was hard to accept while a smattering of letters praising conditions there kept arriving.

For reasons I have never fully understood, while the deportation trains were still rolling in the middle of 1942, the President Tiso instituted a special program then called a "Presidential Exemption." Its purpose was to exclude a very small and carefully selected number of Jews from deportation to the camps. The possession of a coveted "white card" certified one's exemption. That little white piece of cardstock was worth more than gold.

Eligibility for a Presidential Exemption involved an elaborate qualification process, including background checks and verification of one's standing in the community, evidence that one had no more property to yield, and proof that one complied with all conceivable laws and regulations. Most importantly, however, was the ability to claim that one was "economically essential" to the Slovak state. That had to be attested to by a politically prominent sponsor and endorsed by the local Hlinka Guards.

My father had become good friends with a Catholic priest, Monsignor Branecky, while serving on the District Council. Branecky helpfully suggested that baptism would greatly improve our chances of getting a white card. He even offered to personally intervene on my father's behalf with President (and Monsignor) Tiso. Why not?

Catholic baptism is a very arcane and time-consuming process. Too long. My father then turned to another close friend and highly respected Senior (equivalent to Bishop) of the Lutheran Church and arranged for an evangelical baptism so we could be more expeditiously converted to Christianity. Within three months after my bar mitzvah my family started attending classes in catechism to prepare us for a baptism. The event took place early in June, 1942, while the deportations were going strong.

Within weeks my father, my mother, my sister, and I received the wonderful protection of the white card! As a special act of charity, it also applied to my grandparents, which was a matter of uppermost concern to my father.

Baptism

The prospects of undergoing baptism bothered me very little; in these times, one had to do whatever was necessary to survive. Whatever apprehensions my deeply religious mother had were forgotten in the rush to fill out all the necessary forms and conform to all the proper procedures. What made the entire affair easier to accept was that my grandparents did not have to get baptized, even though they would receive all the benefits of the white card protection.

A few other Jews were also "converted"—those who had the connections to manage it. In the spring of 1942, you would have signed your soul over to the devil, if all the devil wanted was a baptismal certificate. And as a bonus, I did not have to wear the yellow star any more. Nevertheless, all of the other restrictive laws on movement, pleasures, subordination, marginal social status, and so forth still applied, because even a baptized Jew was still legally defined as a Jew. That white card provided safety—for a while.

The whole baptism affair involved a great deal of rigmarole. We had to attend catechism, study the Christian religion and its Lutheran variant (the Augsburg Confession), and pass an examination on the finer points of theology separating the Lutherans from other Christian denominations.

In contrast with the Jewish religion, which allowed the widest possible interpretations of its doctrinal substance, the Lutheran heritage focused on the articles of faith, religious conduct, and theological clarity. If you followed the prescribed procedures, attended church on Sundays (including the taking of the sacraments), you were certified as having "done the right thing" and became qualified in the faith. Of course, everyone in the Lutheran community knew this was a charade. By being mostly loyal to the former Czechoslovak state as well as a minority surrounded by the aggressively assertive Catholic Church, the Lutherans viewed the acceptance of the newly-minted Christians as an act of compassion and charity. All I know is that my two years as a Lutheran were characterized by relative peace, and that respite from persecution probably saved my life. Many of the parishioners went out of their way to demonstrate genuine friendship to us, and this despite the madness that was closing in all around.

So far as I know, our conversion was never seen by anyone in our family as a betrayal of our faith and our heritage. My mother never talked about it. I was the only one who attended church with diligence because I found the organ music, psalms, and melodious hymns aesthetically very pleasing. The community singing was inspirational. The Sunday services had an appealing formal structure, which made going to church an interesting weekly experience; one could never guess what the choir or the organist was going to improvise next.

My young evangelical peers were friendly and accepting. They allowed me to assist in organizing puppet theater performances staged every Sunday afternoon for the younger children. I even wrote some theater scripts, along with accompanying musical scores that borrowed generously from Hebrew tunes. The entire group was highly musical and included a number of outstanding pianists and vocalists who delivered a rousing *Messiah* chorus each Easter and Christmas.

Legal Loopholes

After the cessation of deportations in the fall of 1942, the Jewish population in Trenčín was reduced to less than four percent of the prewar count. Because I had been baptized and accepted as a member of the Lutheran Church, I was able to go back to public school. The headmaster was a friend of my father's and this kindly gentleman found a loophole: an enrollment form that did not ask whether one was a Jew. Check marks on the registration forms listed only Christian faiths. I duly noted that I was a Lutheran and thereby complied with the letter of the law while the cooperative officials smiled knowingly. You must understand that such legalistic manipulation was simply a part of life for the Jews; this is how we circumvented many of the lesser annoyances of the bureaucracy.

While in school, I was treated just like all the other students, except for some occasional shoving by a few persistent troublemakers. Everyone knew I was a Jew, but as long as I remained inconspicuous, no one blew my cover. There was, however, one incident (which I was mercifully not present to witness) in which Mr. Hučko, the math professor, became angry with a student who choked on an equation. In his aggravated state, Hučko pointed out that Strassmann, a lower classman, could do it. In response, the humiliated pupil spouted, "It's easy for Strassmann—he's a Jew!"

Our friends the Kubičeks offer an excellent case study in how strict compliance with legal minutiae could save lives. They were transported to the Žilina concentration camp, which was used as a way station to dispatch the weekly trains of death to Auschwitz. Of course everyone was frantically engaged in attempting to find some avenue of escape—a legal loophole. When my father discovered that one of the ways for getting excused from deportation to Auschwitz was a credible claim of American citizenship, he obtained an affidavit signed by the American consul in Portugal (I believe) attesting to the fact that Andrew Kubiček declared his intent to travel with his family to America. A combination of liberal bribes and a claim that this technically qualified the Kubičeks as "Americans" made it possible for them to return to Trenčín where they lived under my father's protection for a while longer.

As you might imagine, the escalating deportations and increasing levels of humiliation caused considerable anxiety and depression in our household. I give my mother much credit for ensuring that a pretense of normality was kept up during these difficult times. I do not recall a single incident in which she quarreled, or even raised her voice, with my father during these trying times.

The only bright moments I can remember during that entire period are episodes in which one of my mother's many friends gave us, or let us buy, eggs, fruit, or cheese. The peasants, many of them former customers of our store, suffered less privation than the city dwellers, who depended upon supplementing food rations with supplies obtained from the black market. Father's access to sources of canned goods and baking ingredients from our store made it possible for Mother to be engaged in endless cooking and baking in her tiny kitchen. Not only was she able to feed our family (and anyone staying with us), but she also managed to produce a steady stream of provisions to be packed up and shipped to friends and relatives in the camps. Whether they ever received these tokens of kindness is another story.

Slum Living

During 1943, we were forced to move again from the relatively decent quarters near the Lutheran church to the only available housing, which was in the town's slum district. Our new apartment was right next to the train tracks and the trains would blast us with their loud whistle whenever they passed. The house did not have running water and we had to use an outdoor privy. The screws were being tightened, but even then that was seen as tolerable.

Much of our time was spent scrounging for food and avoiding every conceivable source of penalties for violating one of the endless rules we were required to follow. By this time, there was no feasible option available for escape. The frontiers and all means of transportation were sealed tight. Besides, with all of Europe occupied by the Germans, there was no place where one could go with an entire family, even illegally.

There was no exit. There were no choices remaining. Staying alive was our only concern. It is only now that I have come to the full realization of the extent to which the Jewish population was transformed from relative prosperity to total impoverishment in less than three years. With very few exceptions, Jews lost their livelihood, property, domiciles, and human dignity. Throughout this ordeal, my father managed to support his family and numerous dependent friends and relatives on the mean salary of an office clerk. As the Nazis were well aware, our lot had become so untenable that the prospect of "resettlement" didn't seem so bad.

End of Deportations

The deportations to Poland ceased suddenly in early September 1942. There is still a great deal of speculation about why this happened. One popular explanation suggests that the Catholic Church intervened after receiving evidence that "resettlement" was a euphemism for genocide. Another story tells of a very large bribe paid directly to Nazi officials by the leadership of the Jewish community. This hypothesis is dubious; why would the Nazis abruptly halt their remarkably efficient murder machine simply to receive funds that they would "inherit" after all the Jews had been done away with? My best guess is that the Slovaks saw that there were no more economic gains to be realized after the Jewish properties had all been seized and reallocated. It is also my opinion that the cash payments by the Slovak Republic to the Nazis for the transfer of custody of the deported Jews left a well-documented trail of culpability for mass murder. This apparently didn't bother the Nazis, but the Slovaks—ever mindful of possible legal ramifications—must have given some thought to the consequences. Their experience with quasi-legal plunder in 1860 and again in 1918 must have taught them lessons in how to ensure that such plunder becomes legitimately acquired property. Finally, the campaign that culminated with the German defeat at Stalingrad—a major turning point in the war—had already begun. Father and I followed the advances (or stasis) of the Wehrmacht every night, marking up a map based on the news reports on the Czechoslovak radio broadcasts from London. I also built an illegal crystal radio that was tuned to track the denials emanating from the local pro-fascist radio station. Repeated denials were always interpreted as a sign that all was not going well for the Germans in Russia.

The Slovak Army had advanced with the Germans to the foothills of the Caucasus Mountains, but by the summer of 1942 it was starting to retreat; some elements were already defecting to the Soviets. As had happened so often in the past, there must have been some thought given to the possibility of reprisals, should fortunes turn. Besides, the remaining Jews in Slovakia were now economically valuable as slave labor. Better that they be kept in productive employment than sacrificed to the Nazi's racist ideology.

As we come to the close of the first stage of the Slovak Holocaust, we are confronted by the following statistics:

> The original Jewish population in the Slovak sector of Czechoslovakia was 89,000, constituting approximately four percent of the total population.
>
> An unaccounted-for portion of the Jews managed to flee. In addition, a part of Slovakia was ceded to Hungary prior to 1940 as part of the Munich Agreement. The best estimate is

> that when the Nazi-sponsored Slovak Republic came into being, the Jewish population of Slovakia was around 79,000.
>
> The number of Slovak Jews deported to death camps in Poland was 59,000. Thanks to the careful accounting for payments from the Slovaks to the Germans, this number is well documented.
>
> About 10,000 of the Slovak Jews were placed in forced labor camps; a few were assigned to auxiliary battalions of the Slovak Army where they were employed in hard labor constructing military installations.
>
> A very small number of Jews disappeared altogether. These ghosts slipped quietly into rural villages where they assumed new identities and acquired false papers. They were the lucky ones.
>
> By September of 1942, the remaining Jewish population in the Slovak Republic was less than 10,000. They were destitute—stripped of their homes, their property, and all civil rights. They were subjected to a regime of degradation and torment.

A small number of the remaining Jews received special privileges that varied according to local conditions. This included Jews of mixed marriages, holders of the coveted "white card" Presidential Exemptions and some families that could claim citizenship (or some sort of a legal connection) to one of the Allied powers (such as the USA and Britain).

Here I have a semantic quibble. One finds frequent references in the Holocaust literature to Nazi "concentration camps." That is a misnomer. A concentration camp was a place where Jews were assembled for further transport to "extermination camps." For instance, Žilina and Sered were used for herding Jews into a controlled space from where they could be transported to extermination camps, such as Auschwitz.

Survivor Stories

Of the 59,000 Slovak Jews deported through 1942, only a handful survived the war. The exact number of these survivors is unknown. I never gave much thought to that until it dawned on me that anyone who survived the horrors of Auschwitz for three years could have accomplished that only by becoming one of the Nazi-appointed lackeys who ran the camps, maintaining discipline among the inmates and managing the distribution of food. It is now a well-documented fact that only a very small SS cadre staffed the extermination camps. By means of organized terror the "processing" of tens of thousands of inmates could be handled only through obedient intermediaries who were granted marginal survival privileges in return for their diligence in engaging in inhumane practices. Although the Nazis preferred to use captive Russian prisoners and Polish criminals for such purposes, they also had to depend on collaborating Jews to fill the ranks of enforcers.

The realization that I must approach all survivor stories with skepticism dawned on me during a flight to Tel Aviv in 1979. I was seated next to a Polish Jew from Frankfurt. The customary introductory question following takeoff was, "Where were you during the war?" This former inmate of Auschwitz proceeded to tell me that he owned large real estate holdings in Frankfurt and had accumulated vast wealth, rising from humble origins as a black marketer selling goods purloined from the American occupation forces. When I inquired about his arrival date in Auschwitz he replied that it was in early 1942. He proudly described how he and his buddies were able to organize themselves for a sort of "self-help" preferential treatment and a better supply of food. He expressed pity for the 1944 arrivals from Slovakia and Hungary who had no "group cohesion" or sense of "organization" and therefore ended up dying "like flies." When I pressed him about the nature of this "self-help," he refused to talk about it, turning the conversation instead to the fact that his name is listed as a major donor to several Holocaust memorials.

In recent years, I have run across many similar cases in which survivors of the camps refused to talk about their experiences. I have encountered Jewish students interested in the history of the Holocaust; they wanted to write essays about it for their college courses, but they could not get a word about those events out of their parents or grandparents. I have never classified myself as a "Holocaust survivor"; rather, I consider myself a talkative "resistance fighter," so the students found it easy to interview me. My message is always that three-year inmates in Auschwitz could only have survived through deeds they would not wish to talk about.

The forms of denial about surviving the war are varied and often amusing. Without exception, every German executive I met during my years as an information technology specialist for large US corporations (General Foods, Kraft, and Xerox) made sure that during the obligatory dinner parties held for visiting executives, they sought me out—the sole Jew in the group—and offered the benign acknowledgement that they had whiled away the war as low-level officers in German Army antiaircraft defense forces.

Another Option for Slovaks?[10]

In May 2003 I was asked to chair the Federal Holocaust Remembrance Day in Washington, D.C. This is an annual event, and that year it was devoted to a celebration of how the Bulgarians had saved their Jewish citizens.

Bulgaria had a population of more than six million people in 1934. In that year, Jews constituted 0.8 percent of the total population, or roughly 50,000 individuals. In terms of the ratio of Jews to non-Jews, that was comparable to Slovakia.

In early March 1941, Bulgaria joined the Axis alliance and the following month participated in the German-led attack on Yugoslavia and Greece. In return, Bulgaria received most of Thrace and Macedonia as well as parts of eastern Serbia. Although Bulgaria participated in the Balkan military campaign in support of Germany, it refused to enter the war against the Soviet Union in June 1941.

Beginning in July 1940, Bulgaria instituted anti-Jewish legislation, as dictated by the Germans. Jews were excluded from public service, dis-

[10]Source for this chapter is the *Holocaust Encyclopedia*, U.S. Holocaust Museum.

criminated against in their choice of housing, and restricted economically. Marriage between Jews and non-Jews was prohibited.

Germany-allied Bulgaria did not deport their Jews. They did, however, deport non-Bulgarian Jews from the territories they had annexed from Yugoslavia and Greece. Jews of Bulgarian citizenship remained secure from deportation to German-held territory. Nevertheless, Bulgarian Jewish men between the ages of twenty and forty were dragooned into forced labor, and in May 1943, the Bulgarian government announced the expulsion of 20,000 Jews from Sofia to the provinces. Around this same time, the Bulgarian government also made extensive plans to comply with the Nazi insistence that deportation of Bulgaria's Jews to Poland commence immediately. Protests from leading political and clerical leaders moved King Boris to cancel these deportation plans.

In 1945, the Jewish population of Bulgaria remained about the same as its prewar level. Next to the rescue of Danish Jews, Bulgarian Jewry's escape from deportation and extermination represents the most significant exception of any Jewish population in Nazi-occupied Europe. That is worthy of celebration!

Bulgaria's hardline stance against forsaking its Jewish community to appease the Nazis is one of the more remarkable stories of World War II and one of the least known. This is not to say that the Jews were not affected by the threat of deportation; twice deportations were ordered, but in the end no Bulgarian Jew was sent to the death camps.

Several forces combined to save the Bulgarian Jewish community. The Bulgarian Eastern Orthodox Church was especially honorable in this regard, probably more than any other religious organization in Europe. It worked (both in public and private) on behalf of Bulgarian Jews. The Bulgarian attitude of religious tolerance was reflected in the fact that Jews, Christians, and Muslims had lived in harmony for centuries. In the northern part of the country, farmers threatened to lie down on the tracks to stop trains bearing human cargo.

The Bulgarian vs. Slovak Statistics

Bulgarian prewar Jewish population: 50,000; Postwar Jews: 50,000.

Slovak prewar Jewish population: 79,000; Postwar Jews: 6,400.

Bulgarian Army: Attacked Germans with Soviet Army support. Successful.

Slovak Army: Attacked Germans without Soviet Army support. Failure.

THE MILITARY

There were two principal Slovak resistance movements, and both had various splinter factions. One operated out of London under the auspices of the legitimate Czechoslovak government in exile. This group was relying on Anglo-American political support to reestablish the prewar Czechoslovak Republic. The other outfit was a Communist anti-fascist organization that took its orders from Moscow and fell under the purview of the Comintern (the global Communist coordination agency).

Both groups began maneuvering for the postwar assumption of power as early as 1942. The military goal set by the London-based command was to allow the Soviet Army to sweep west without destroying the towns and villages in Czechoslovakia. By 1944, the devastation of Russia—first by the retreating Soviets in 1941, then by the retreating Germans, and again by the advancing Soviets—made it clear that Czechoslovakia was likely to finish the war as a ravaged countryside. The Communist Party set its own military goals: Its primary objective was to reconstitute Czechoslovakia as a Soviet satellite.

The Slovak Army

In 1944, the Slovak Army was a formidable force for a country of only four million citizens. The active duty forces comprised two divisions of 37,000 men with an additional 15,000 reserves available for mobilization on short notice. Only one of these divisions (based in eastern Slovakia) was combat-ready. It had 300 heavy artillery pieces, fifty tanks, forty-two airplanes, and 100 antiaircraft guns at its disposal, and it boasted well-protected and fully stocked arsenals for ammunition, auxiliary supplies, and fuel. Almost all of these armaments were left over from the once powerful Czechoslovak Army when it disintegrated in 1938. A second division (based in western Slovakia) consisted primarily of troops for logistical support (transportation, communication, medical, and training) of the front-line contingent.

The Slovak Army participated in the German invasion of Poland in 1939—the blitzkrieg operation that initiated World War II. In fact, Slovakia was the only Nazi ally that participated in that action. In 1941, both Slovak divisions also supported the German offensive against the Soviets; Slovak troops were among those penetrating deepest into the foothills of the Caucasus Mountains. Slovak officers witnessed the desolation that characterized the war on the Eastern Front; the idea that Slovakia could ultimately become such a battleground must have been in the back of their minds. They knew they were risking brutal reprisals should the fortunes of the Axis shift, leaving the Soviets in possession of Slovakia and primed for retribution.

There was much dissension in the ranks of the Slovak Army; the troops and their leaders saw that the Germans were not invincible, and many Slovaks sought an opportunity to defect. This mindset was not lost on the Allies, and in early 1944 the London-based Czechoslovak minister of defense hatched a scheme to turn the well-armed Slovak Army divisions (now withdrawn from the Soviet front by the Germans as being unreliable) into turncoats. The Allied plan involved launching a vicious attack from the rear on the Germans defending the Dukla Pass in Carpathian Mountains. The idea was to bottle the Germans up in the pass, thus allowing the Soviet forces to sweep through Slovakia and establish a relatively speedy occupation. Such a plan called for an organized armed uprising of the Slovak Army that would be supported by the Allies. Specific commitments were difficult to ascertain because all activity on the Eastern Front was controlled by the Soviets. A few agents (officers from the Czechoslovak Army now in England) started arriving in Slovakia to meet with their Slovak Army counterparts.

It is not my purpose to dwell on the muddled history of how the Slovak National Uprising was planned, initiated, executed, bungled, and finally put down. There is an enormous collection of books, essays, and documents offering contradictory interpretations of frequently unverifiable facts. I will leave the untangling of the evidence to historians who will pick over the extant documentation and debate about what really happened for decades to come. The best I can do here is to tell the story the best way I know how from bits and scraps of conversations with those who were there.

Preparing for the Uprising

My father, who indirectly controlled much of the food distribution in the strategic Trenčín district, was party to moving a large quantity of food from regional depots to the village stores in the surrounding mountains in early 1944. The excuse was this: If the predictions of a severe winter came to pass, the village stores must increase their inventories now, as the mountain roads could become virtually impassable and gasoline was becoming a scarce commodity.

The effort to cache food coincided with actions initiated by cooperating government officials who began to lay the groundwork for the coming revolt. Years later I found out that what Father was doing was but a small part of much larger operation involving the following:

> Moving three months of food supply to the central region where the uprising would be concentrated.
>
> Transferring money reserves as well as the gold reserves from the Slovak central bank to the central region.[11]
>
> Hiding 1.3 million liters of gasoline in mountain depots.
>
> Surreptitiously relocating the entire army medical corps from the capital of Slovakia to the central region.

[11]When the Slovak National Uprising collapsed, the Soviet high command saw to it that the gold—and not the wounded—was evacuated on the last flights out to Kiev.

Such activities could not remain hidden from the ever-present agents of the Gestapo and the Slovak Hlinka Guard informers. For the planners of the uprising to assume that a coup could come as a complete surprise was laughable. This error in planning assumptions and in a faulty intelligence unfolded into a series of erroneous decisions that ultimately doomed the uprising.

Perhaps the greatest fault in planning the uprising was a lack of flexibility; key leaders failed to modify the original operational plans as they continued to receive conflicting and contradictory guidance from London, which was further altered by Moscow.

War and Politics

The directives from London were simple. First, under no circumstances should the Slovak Army initiate the uprising until the Soviets were ready to cross the Carpathian passes from Poland and the Ukraine through Slovakia on their way to Budapest and Vienna. Only after the Soviet command gave the signal to proceed would the Slovak Army have any chance of survival. Second, since the Germans would not permit the Slovaks to retain the initiative once they had shown their cards, the Wehrmacht would occupy Slovakia on the slightest provocation to protect its logistical resources. In such an event, the Slovak Army would have to disengage and take to the hills. They would then be forced to conduct *partizán* warfare, as had been successfully demonstrated in Yugoslavia.

The operational guidance issued from the political command in Kiev was designed to inflict the greatest damage and the most severe casualties on the Slovak forces. They would in essence be sacrificed in a diversionary action that would give the Soviets the freedom to liberate as much Slovak territory as they felt they could hold against a counterattack. The encircled Slovaks would have to hold until the Soviet Army arrived. This plan was based on the premise that whatever the military outcome, political control of the region would fall to the Communist Party. The Soviet "liberators" would become the de facto rulers of Slovakia.

The Kiev directive was in direct contradiction to the tactical plans of the First Ukrainian Army (Marshall Konev), the Second Ukrainian

Army (General Malinowski) and the Fourth Ukrainian Army (General Petrov). The attack plans in the Soviet archives reveal that these commanders did not contemplate any fighting in the mountainous regions of central Slovakia, where the uprising was ultimately concentrated. Instead, the thrust of the Soviet advance was aimed at the open plains, where their mechanized infantry and massed artillery barrages could easily defeat any German attempt at a counterattack.

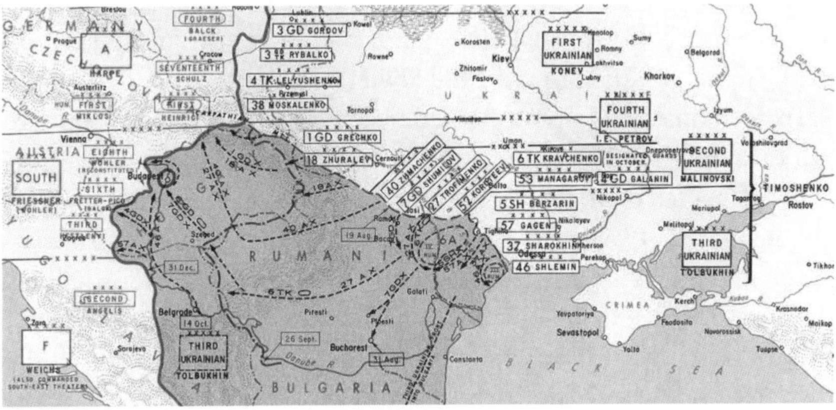

24. Soviet Battle Lines, 8/19/44 to 12/31/44[12]

The Kiev plan reflected recommendations originally presented to Stalin at a conference in Moscow early in 1942 by Georgi Dimitroff, the head of the Comintern. In 1943, Stalin assigned the job of steering the resistance movements in Eastern Europe to his troubleshooter commissar, Nikita Khrushchev. A headquarters element was established in Kiev in early 1944 with full authority to oversee *partizán* operations in occupied countries.

[12]U.S. Military Academy, West Point, is the source of this map of the Soviet Southern command. See http://www.dean.usma.edu/history/web03/atlases/ww2%20europe/ww2%20europe%20pages/ww2%20europe%20map%2030.htm. The heavy line shows the position as of 12/31/1944 and confirms that the front lines remained stagnant from 8/19/1944, except where the Soviets exploited the switching of the Rumanian, Bulgarian, and Hungarian armies from German to Allied allegiance (see the shaded area). The main thrust of the armies under Marshall Timoshenko was aimed along the Danube plain. Meanwhile the Slovak participants in the uprising were led to believe that liberation was imminent.

The *Partizán* Role

Guidance from the Soviet command was strictly operational: *Partizán* warfare was to commence in June of 1944 with the airborne insertion of ten commando teams in mountainous spots near railroad lines that ran on a north-south axis through the Carpathian Mountains.

In the early months of 1944, the German high command was still trying to guess whether the main Soviet attack would come through the heavily defended northern Polish plain or the southern Danube basin. Since the battle of Kursk in 1943, the Soviet Army had depended on a massive armored onslaught accompanied by concentrated artillery barrages to punch through the German defenses—enormous casualties were immaterial (and expected). Therefore, the next attack would have to roll through the plains and not over the mountain range where defensible positions could be set up against any thrusts launched on east-west coordinates.

As the Soviet military command saw it, the purpose of any *partizán* actions would primarily be to interfere with the Germans' ability to shift troops and panzers to the north or south. The Soviet-led Slovak *partizáns* teams would also divert German resources from the front lines to protect their supply lines. Disruptions in the rail traffic in particular would wreak havoc on the Germans' ability to rapidly redeploy precious military reserves.

The Soviets viewed the *partizáns* as an expendable resource—use them as necessary and throw them away. This attitude was reinforced by the NKVD—the commissars who spied on the army commanders and who viewed all *partizáns* as operationally suspect and politically untrustworthy. Such bias became obvious when my *partizán* unit finally crossed the front lines in March 1945. The Slovaks were automatically transferred to the Czechoslovak Army for security screening to weed out any possible infiltrators. Our Russian *partizáns* were handed over to the NKVD who "disappeared" them into the gulag system, regardless of their combat record.

As the situation evolved, the conventional Soviet military role assumed a secondary priority while *partizán* tactics were implemented with reasonable competence and success. Our irregular activities were comparatively small in the overall scheme of things and didn't make that much of a difference to the outcome of the war in Slovakia; still, they saved my life.

The political objectives pursued by the *partizán* headquarters in Kiev ultimately prevailed. As the tragedy unfolded, the Slovak Army ignored the directives from London. And when the uprising was triggered prematurely, the Slovak Army reverted to suicidal conventional military tactics. Civilian authorities from Moscow and London tried to assert control over the Slovak military during the few weeks in which there was a liberated territory, but the internal conflicts worsened. Without any coherent leadership or a unifying strategy, the uprising was doomed to failure.

Under such circumstances, the resistance fighters fractured into small bands, each pursuing its own salvation. To complicate matters further, the country was awash with refugees of every stripe: Jews liberated from labor camps, Tiso regime turncoats trying to save their own skin, liberated POWs, convicts on the lam, British intelligence operatives, an American OSS team, Jewish agents from Palestine, downed American pilots, German anti-Nazis, gypsies, and scores of others were all wandering about, looking for ways to survive.

The Best-Laid Plans ...

A secret Slovak Revolutionary Council meeting attended by representatives of the major prewar political parties as well as the Communists was held in late May of 1944 in western Slovakia. The delegates agreed that an uprising of the Slovak Army would initiate the campaign and act as a diversion allowing the Soviets to push through the Carpathian Mountains and liberate large swathes of Slovakia with dispatch and minimal civilian casualties. A military operation of this nature depended upon the element of surprise to have any hope for success. Timing, too, would be of the utmost importance. Perfect coordination of the Slovak Army uprising, the Soviet Army assault, and the *partizán* diversionary strikes was essential; reliable communications between these elements would prove critical. The Soviet thrust across the Carpathians would have to be channeled along the three passes through these imposing mountains—they were a defender's dream. The Slovak Army was presumed to hold the initial tactical advantage, because at the time the plans were laid there were no German combat troops in Slovakia.

The assumption that the Soviets would share their battle plans with the Slovak Army command was patently unrealistic. So far as the Communists were concerned, as former Nazi allies, the Slovak officers were traitors; if it had been up to them, the Slovak commanders would have been executed. Therefore, a joint Soviet–Slovak operation was an improbable scenario at best. Not a very good start.

As any messages from a Slovak Army officer were considered tainted, a Slovak civilian named Villiam Široky was selected to act as liaison between the Slovak Army and the Soviets. Široky seemed a logical choice for the assignment: A member of the Slovak Communist Party underground politburo, he claimed to already be in radio contact with the political command at the Kiev *partizán* headquarters. But after a month in which Široky made no contact with the Soviets whatsoever, he alleged that his equipment had apparently malfunctioned and offered to communicate with Khrushchev personally. The future chairman of the Soviet Politburo was an important player in this drama, as he was in charge of the political wing of the *partizán* command. It was his job to ensure that Czechoslovakia became a Soviet possession after the war. Khrushchev had no orders or mandate to cooperate with the Slovak Army.

Široky was ferried to Kiev in a hill-dodging observation biplane, and he promptly disappeared without a trace for several months, leaving Slovak military planners in a near-panic state. Relying on a Communist Party officer whose allegiance was to the political rather than the military was a terrible mistake. So far as I am concerned, it was Široky who undermined the uprising even before it began. For his service as a faithful Communist, Široky was appointed prime minister of Czechoslovakia after the Communists took over in 1948. Široky then presided over a series of show trials and purges of prewar Communist Party idealists, including party leaders who fought in the Slovak National Uprising and who could (and sometimes did) point to his role as the spoiler of anti-Nazi resistance.

From the very beginning, it must have been clear to military planners in London and Moscow that the Soviet Army needn't slog its way through the Carpathian Mountains to achieve the prime objective—the concentration and destruction of the German forces progressively retreating to engage in the final defense of Berlin.

The demonstration in the Dukla Pass was merely a feint designed to allow the Soviet mechanized juggernaut to pour through the Danube plain relatively unmolested. There was no need for the Soviet tanks and artillery to turn east and grind their way through the treacherous mountain passes where the uprising was to be staged. The hazardous job of plugging the Dukla Pass was assigned to the newly-formed Czechoslovak corps comprising deserters from the Slovak Army and patriots who had somehow survived the war by escaping to Moscow in 1939—a tall order for a combat-hardened veteran unit, let alone an untested outfit with little cohesion.

I have to digress here for a moment to explain that in the summer of 1947 I hiked through one of the passes in the Carpathian Mountains. The view took my breath away, as I surveyed the succession of barren hillsides surrounding the winding narrow road leading from Poland to Slovakia northeast of Žilina. It was readily apparent that the pass could be easily defended by a relatively small number of well-positioned gun emplacements with only token infantry support. Neutralizing these positions would require uphill charges by massed infantry over open pastureland with no cover whatsoever. Furthermore, the hills would have to be assaulted in daylight to enable the close artillery support favored by the Soviets. Their troops did not fight at night—only the *partizáns* did so. The local peasants regaled me with tales of the enormous casualties suffered by the Soviet infantry charging against dug-in positions during the final phase of the war—a time when occupying the mountain passes was militarily irrelevant.

Communist Conspiracy?

It should have been also clear to the planners of the uprising that the Soviet political command had no motivation to support a military coup mounted by Slovak officers who were being steered by the pro-democratic Slovak government-in-exile in London. Stalin had no desire to sponsor a successful uprising by an army that was ideologically beholden to the

West, that had served under a fascist administration, that repeatedly displayed allegiance to the Catholic faith, and that had successfully fought against the Soviets in prior years.

With the benefit of hindsight, we can see that the Slovak uprising was doomed before it began. It was predicated on faulty assumptions about the capabilities of the German Army. The Slovak officers who planned to engage in what was in fact a mutiny had no fallback plan in case the Germans responded with overwhelming force—a reaction that was given a high probability. Without the carefully coordinated support of the Soviets, the uprising would surely meet the fate of the Polish Home Army in Warsaw in 1944. In the Warsaw uprising, the Soviets who were supposed to reinforce the insurgents halted their advance a few miles short of the area where the Poles were being massacred by SS counterinsurgency forces.[13] Also, the presumption of attaining the element of surprise was ludicrous. German intelligence was monitoring the operation all along. Despite all of these fatal flaws, the planning of the carefully orchestrated defection of the Slovak Army continued throughout the summer. Unfortunately, the architects of the plan in London and Moscow had virtually no control over events on the ground, and the premature triggering of the Slovak National Uprising on August 28, 1944, was the last nail in its coffin.

Whether the Slovak Army revolt was the victim of poor planning and execution or compromised by a clever Communist-inspired conspiracy will never be known. It really doesn't matter. We do know that it was the rash action of a Soviet commando team that set off the chain of events resulting in the precipitate launch of the uprising. I personally find the possibility of a Communist conspiracy to be plausible. Still, the numerous missteps in organization and blatant incompetence in leadership must have contributed to the disaster.

Triggering the Uprising

On the night of the twenty-fifth of August, a small group of men boarded a passenger train at a remote station. The train was returning from

[13]When they finished their killing spree in Poland, these specialized units (known as SS Battle Group Schill) were immediately deployed to Slovakia to perform a similar job.

Bucharest to Berlin, and the stop was only made to resupply the water for the boiler before the climb through the Carpathian Mountains. The men were in fact members of a Soviet commando team that had been parachuted into Slovakia a month before. It is not clear why the team indulged in this unorthodox behavior; my view is that they intended to rob the passengers. The Soviets came from a devastated land and had never seen such prosperity, and sometimes it was just too much temptation. They were particularly crazy about acquiring wristwatches and anything made of gold. To the interlopers' surprise, they discovered that sleeping cars were full of German general staff officers and their deputies returning from a meeting in Bucharest. Without revealing their identity, the Soviets took custody of the Germans and handed them over to the Slovak Army at the next stop (per previously established rules).

The Germans were understandably miffed at this kind of undignified treatment, but as the Slovak Army was an Axis ally, they had no reason to suspect anything was amiss. They were of course allowed to keep their weapons while being escorted to the nearby barracks where they were provided with quarters for the night. The local Slovak commander was under strict orders from Lieutenant Colonel Golian, now the titular head of the planned uprising, to make sure that no harm came to any captured Germans, as that would surely invite countermeasures and possibly blow the entire operation.

The German officers fell in on the parade ground in for the customary morning formation. A single shot ruptured the morning stillness and a German officer collapsed in a heap. Being armed, the Germans proceeded to defend themselves, but Slovak machine guns mowed them down. Whether some anonymous trigger-happy Slovak or a Soviet agent provocateur fired the shot that instigated the massacre remains unknown.

What Happened?

There are many versions of what happened that morning. My own speculation is colored by my experiences as a member of a Soviet-led *partizán* squad that was organized and controlled exactly as the one that stopped the train and detained the German officers. We were under strict orders to avoid engagement with the Germans or their support troops because direct combat was not our mission. We were essentially a demolition team, and our mission was to interdict rail traffic. Firefights would only result in reprisals against the civilian population and provide an added incentive to hunt us down. If we did our job well, the enemy would never even see us.

The handling of the German detainees by the Russian commandos was consistent with our own orders. Dealing with prisoners was not our job. So barring a meticulously planned covert operation in which the Russian commandos played their part to a 'T' (so the blame would be placed on the Slovaks), or a Nazi-inspired assassination that would justify them in ordering the Slovak Army to stand down (thus derailing the anticipated uprising), I am of the opinion that it was just a stupid mistake. History is full of them.

When it comes to understanding military and political matters, I embrace the old maxim: "Do not look for a conspiracy when incompetence can explain it all."

Slipshod Uprising

Immediately after the news of the massacre leaked out, the Gestapo proceeded to implement preplanned countermeasures that called for the disarming of the Slovak Army to circumvent the uprising. If it had not ordered the assassination operation, the German high command must have surmised that the execution of the officers was the signal for the uprising to begin. In any event, the incident provided the Germans with all the justification they needed to come down hard on the Slovaks—and punitive operations were one of their favorite pastimes.

The undermanned Gestapo and the limited number of SS-police troops in the area were insufficient to disarm the Slovak Army in the western part of Slovakia (whose headquarters were in Trenčín). The lower-ranking stratum of the officer corps had been preparing for a mutiny anyway; these ambitious fellows were eager to hook up with the winning side and salvage their careers, so they joined in with gusto. In the resulting small-scale scuffles, the Nazis were overwhelmed. Meanwhile, a radio station in Banská Bystrica fell under the control of a radical faction and broadcast the news that the uprising had started.

Though they were late to the party, the genuine conspirators finally set their plan in motion. On the morning of August 29, 1944, Lieutenant Colonel Golian finally issued the belated signal to commence the uprising. Subsequent political developments wrested control of events out of the hands of the Slovak military and into the iron fist of the Communist leadership. Though the Soviets retained political control, responsibility (and eventually, blame) for the execution of all military actions was placed on a small cadre of Slovak officers.

The Roots of Failure

The original plans depended on the combat-ready Slovak Army division located in the eastern part of Slovakia to join the uprising. This 15,000-man division was adequately equipped with heavy weapons to seize and hold Dukla Pass until the Soviets arrived with reinforcements. The commander of the eastern contingent, General August Malar, demanded to see orders assuring the coordination of Soviet movements with his own. The headquarters for the insurgency in Banská Bystrica could not provide such orders, so Malar refused to commit his troops. The undermanned operations center did its best to appease Malar, but no communication link between the Slovak general and the Soviet command was ever established. While Malar sat tight, a relatively small contingent of German troops arrived on the scene and disarmed Malar's soldiers without firing a shot. Any chance the uprising might have had for success vanished into thin air.

The unfolding of the uprising in the western part of Slovakia showed mixed results. Individual units of the Slovak Army defected from their local garrisons in small units but not under a unified command. These were reserve troops with little combat experience, and no armaments capable of resisting seasoned German mechanized infantry supported by panzers and close air support. In the absence of a clear chain of command, about half of the soldiers deserted and returned home, where they changed into civilian clothing and quietly went about their business. Some remained loyal to the Tiso regime—for example, the 2,000-man Nitra garrison supported the SS in attacking uniformed Slovak Army units that were in open revolt.

The fact that a general (for Golian had been promoted) reporting to the London-based Slovak government was leading the uprising assured the reticence of the Soviets. The Communists who repatriated from their Moscow exile concentrated on asserting political control over the government in the liberated territories instead of building adequate defenses. There was a major power play going on while the Huns were knocking on the door.

The (presumably) unintended initiation of the Slovak National Uprising hinged on a regrettable mistake. That incident toppled the first of many dominos. The unintended consequences of the assassination of the German officers by a handful of soldiers were a series of events that soon involved over 100,000 combatants and affected perhaps a million innocent civilians. Students of history and politics can readily see how many small errors can accumulate and escalate, yielding unexpected outcomes. Perhaps the principal reason why these events took uncontrollable turns was the absence of networked communications. The stakeholders in the uprising—the exiled government in London, the Moscow Communist apparatchiks, the Soviet *partizán* command in Kiev, the Soviet military commanders on the ground, and at least two different Slovak Army factions, did not and could not communicate rapidly because they had neither the technical means nor the political and/or operational will to do so. There would be no cooperation in this bungled mission.

The various actors in this tragedy pursued divergent political agendas and military objectives even though they were unified in fighting the Nazis. The end of the war was in sight and the contest for claiming territory and assuming postwar powers had already begun, even though reality dictated the need to focus on defeating the Nazis first. When the emissaries from the British SOE and American OSS landed in mid-September for liaison and observation purposes, they could only stand by and watch as the doomed military adventure spiraled inexorably toward failure.

Nazi Retribution

In the pursuit of "damage control," the local Gestapo and collaborators proceeded to execute a plan of their own. During the night of August 28, they raided the homes of the key suspects in towns where there were army bases, with the divisional headquarters in Trenčín receiving top priority. My father was arrested in the initial roundup. He was interrogated and severely beaten. The man in charge of the abduction was a young Slovak by the name of Kraus who had recently joined a Nazi auxiliary that consisted of men claiming to be of German origin. Kraus was the educated son of a prominent local architect who knew my father well. When armed violence was unleashed by the uprising, the response by the pro-Nazi faithful was to indiscriminately apply a level of brutality generally reserved for "bandits" and "terrorists," but this time the Jews were singled out for exceptional cruelty.

Desperate Situation

By the second week in September of 1944, probing skirmishes took place using undermanned counterinsurgency SS police. The Germans started their punitive expedition with raids on a few enclaves where deserters hid out in western Slovakia. They were often confounded by those who knew well how to construct defensive positions. In one instance, a group of French Army POWs landed in Slovakia at the start of the uprising when a freight train upon which they were being transported was intercepted by Slovak *partizáns.* With armory doors thrown open, these erstwhile prisoners organized themselves into a cohesive and highly-motivated fighting force. They demolished a German unit in a narrow mountain pass with only small arms. The German counterinsurgency troops quickly determined that heavier attack forces would be needed to root out the remnants of an army that were digging in to fixed positions. The SS also applied terror—its favorite weapon of choice—where the unarmed populace was in no position to resist.

During this period, wholesale executions took place; these were mostly Jews who were simply seeking a refuge from the violence. Immediately after the start of the revolt, the area covered by the reincarnated Czechoslovak state was about 100 by 250 miles. That area started shrinking with the initial probing attacks of the resurgent German forces. The Slovak Army, trained for conventional warfare, kept withdrawing into more defensible mountainous districts anchored on the town of Banská Bystrica. Prospects of connecting with the Soviets advancing over the Carpathian Mountains were becoming slimmer by the day, and the morale of the Slovak troops was flagging; they knew they could not hold out for long with Soviet support. With few exceptions, when the Germans launched an assault, the defenders fled. It was just a matter of time before the German panzers, supported by the dreaded *Stuka* dive bombers, closed in on the steadily shrinking territory and drove the remaining forces into the mountains. Resistance was disintegrating.

By mid-October, elite SS troops—including the division that had just eliminated the Polish Home Army in the Warsaw Uprising—started arriving in Slovakia. Capitalizing on good intelligence, the Germans maneuvered into position for a coordinated assault on Banská Bystrica, the heart of what remained of "liberated Czechoslovakia."

With the political elements and military forces backing the uprising concentrated in one location (one of many errors), the Germans were poised to decapitate the central command in a single, swift blow. The capture of the rebel capital would also deny the remaining insurgents access to Tri Duby, the only airfield in its territory, eliminating the possibility of Allied logistical support.

The loss of Banská Bystrica signaled the end of the uprising. Sustaining a large liberated territory 300 kilometers behind the front lines was simply not feasible. Political squabbling between the Communists in Moscow and the London leadership resulted in contradictory strategic guidance, there was no coordinated command and control, and the insurgents were hopelessly outgunned—they had no armor assets and no air cover. By October 28, 1944, the last traces of "liberated Czechoslovakia" had been wiped out. Slovak Army soldiers tried to melt away into their native villages. Those who were caught were shipped to camps in Germany where they were treated as outlaws rather than prisoners of war. With the exception of the *partizáns* (completely under Soviet command) and a few remnants of the Czechoslovak resistance the uprising was finished.

No Shoes

Five weeks after the last remaining territory of liberated Czechoslovakia fell to the Nazis, my partizán squad had to pass over a section of a road north of Donovaly over which the Slovak soldiers' withdrawal had taken place. Although the ground was already covered with snow, the chaos of the retreat was everywhere evident: We passed piles of helmets, backpacks, ammunition crates, burnt-out vehicles, abandoned antiaircraft guns, and bullet-riddled ambulances. Though we were warned about booby-traps, we managed to salvage many frozen uniforms (and they came in handy, as our own garments were in a deplorable state). No shoes or boots could be found. It was apparent that the fleeing Slovak soldiers were shedding vestiges of a military appearance. They must have changed into civilian clothes as they walked back home.

In the Wake of the Uprising

Most of the German troops withdrew from Slovakia immediately after the neutralization of the uprising and returned to the battleground that was now taking shape in the Polish plain. They left police troops, composed mainly of ex-Soviet prisoners of war of Ukrainian, Lithuanian, and Latvian descent who had been commissioned by the SS to act as executioners. These troops were highly skilled in counterinsurgency warfare. The SS-police troops were brutally efficient and employed raid tactics that were indistinguishable from the methods used by Soviet partizáns. Their favorite ruse was to put on clothing that made them look like they were Slovak partizáns. In one instance, they strolled boldly into a partizán encampment talking loudly in Russian and proceeded to cut everyone down with machine-gun bursts. Using such ruses, they often managed to flush out Jews or civilians who were hiding and revealed themselves to seek assistance. The duped victims were tortured to betray others and then murdered on the spot.

During mop-up operations in the wake of the Slovak uprising, the SS took 19,000 military prisoners of whom 5,000 were Jews. The Hlinka Guards then devoted their efforts to capturing all the remaining Jews, with an estimate that 13,500 more were deported. No more than 5,000 Slovakian Jews remained in the country, and they were either hiding out, living under false identities, or fighting with the partizáns.

A Better Way

The ineffective and subsequently failed Slovak uprising must be viewed in the context of actions taken by other German military allies:

On August 25, 1944, the Rumanian government declared war on Germany. Its army aligned with the Soviets in the drive west and ended up occupying parts of Slovakia. The Rumanian switch took place smoothly and with hardly any retaliation from the Germans. The civilian populace did not suffer from being thrust into the midst of a combat zone.

On September 8, 1944, Bulgaria followed suit and declared war on Germany. The Bulgarians also linked up with the Soviets and occupied the entire country, without unnecessary destruction of towns and villages. This swift and well-executed reversal in allegiance avoided civilian casualties and saved the lives of every Jew in Bulgaria.

On October 15, 1944, Hungary announced the end of hostilities against the Allies. Three days later, the Hungarian Army partnered with the Soviets in attacks on German positions. Lives and property were certainly saved.

This remarkable record of rapidly and efficiently recasting German supporters into Allied forces is critically important to understand in rendering a judgment about the bungled Slovak uprising. In my view, it took exceptional incompetence to create the mess in Slovakia.

The actions of the Slovak Army should be compared to those taken by the Rumanians, Bulgarians, and Hungarians. In each case, the switch from the losing side to the winning side took place almost simultaneously with the defection of the Slovak Army. It is probable that my family—and countless others—could have been saved had it not been for the arrogant disregard of military and political realities by the Slovak leadership.

The Jewish Legacy to Humanity

The sequence of subjugation that began in 1938 with the deprivation of civil rights and the confiscation of property, and continued to escalate until the Nazis abducted and beat my father and carted him off to an extermination camp in September of 1944 carved a deep imprint on my consciousness. It gave me an insight into how thin is the veneer over what we grandly term "civilization." It led me down a path of inquiry to attempt to comprehend the dynamics of the progress that has been made from primitive savagery to the current stages of evolution. After witnessing the disintegration of the social fabric of Slovakia, I developed a lifetime compulsion to understand what prevents any society from tearing itself asunder whenever the frail tissue of civility is removed.

After many years of searching (and enjoying the good fortune of living in peace in America), I came to define human freedom as the capacity of a community to offer a predictable expectation that justice will prevail at all times, for all people. For freedom to exist, one must follow the path delineated by that quintessential milestone of humane civilization, the Ten Commandments. These guidelines embody a heritage passed from the Jews to all mankind, a legacy that no persecution can expunge.

The crimes against my family began with a disregard of their rights as citizens, rights that were accorded to all other Slovaks. Such injustice was compounded by a series of laws that progressively denied their existence as human beings. Finally, the injustice culminated in violations, some even perpetrated by devoutly religious Slovaks, of God's laws. Whereas injustice could be disguised before the Slovak population by the legalistic charades from 1938 through 1942 (when the actual killing was subcontracted to the Nazi death factories), after that period the Slovak government and the Hlinka Guards could no longer wash the blood from their hands. When the time came to enact the Final Solution in 1944, all pretenses of legality were dispensed with.

It is the horror of wars that they break down the rules that sustain civil order and replace them with a regression to a time when life was primitive and brutal, kill or be killed.

Fight When You Must!

The Jewish *partizáns* had no place to go. Consequently, the ratio of Jews to all others remaining in combat service widened after the end of October. The survival rate of the non-Jewish partizáns, mostly ex-soldiers and our veteran Russian leaders, was better than that of the Jewish partizáns. By this time, Jewish combatants had determined never to be captured, so they took heavier casualties. Even so, of the 2,000 or so Jews who joined the *partizáns* (including 200 women), only about 500 died in combat. So 75 percent of those who fought survived. All things considered, our odds of survival were certainly better than those who were captured or deported to camps.

In guerrilla warfare, attitude and capabilities are more important than just the numerical odds in keeping one alive. Most of those deported to death camps were people to whom the concept of guerrilla fighting was alien. They were people with no prior experience in how to hide and survive in a hostile countryside. Most had never even held a firearm. Even when guns became widely available during the early stages of the uprising, most of the Jews sought hiding places rather than arms.

The fear that had been instilled in the Jews during the prior five years deterred them from taking any action that could be construed as "illegal." The Jewish religious leadership who followed the "learn how to submit" traditions promoted much of this passivity. Thus most of the adult Jews, even able-bodied men, simply could not bring themselves to consider armed resistance as a viable survival choice.

I am sure that many readers will find my judgment about the lack of the will to fight insensitive to the circumstances and to the prevailing cultural biases of the Jewish community in Slovakia. I will admit that in addition to my own combat experience, my views in this regard have been tempered by my exposure to American and Israeli philosophies regarding the right, the *obligation*, of self-defense. The fiction of passive compliance as the preferable path to survival was shattered forever in early 1944, when two Jews who had escaped from the Auschwitz extermination camp provided eyewitness testimony to the mass murder being ruthlessly and efficiently conducted there.

So far as I know, none of the rabbis who debriefed escapees and compiled comprehensive reports about genocide for transmission to the Allies, promoted a campaign to encourage Jews to protect themselves by dispersing into villages, sheds, or other hideouts. Places that were far away from urban centers, military bases, potential defensive strong points, or major transportation hubs offered a more sustainable refuge during the months (or weeks) in which the terminal phase of the war was being prosecuted. Instead, with only a few exceptions Jews continued to maintain a sense of what they then considered as normalcy. As the end of the war approached, the Jews were concentrated in urban centers where they would be most vulnerable to instant capture and deportation. To the rabbis, consciously taking evasive action would have been alien to most Jews and counter to the experience acquired through centuries of persecution. This view is inexcusable, because they were not dealing with "persecution," rather, they were faced with the prospect of almost certain death as the retreating and desperate Germans would surely do everything in their power to wipe out all remaining traces of European Jewry.

I am convinced that the survival rate of the more than 20,000 Jews who were still in Slovakia at the beginning of the uprising would have been much better if they had been willing to choose dispersal and, if necessary, armed resistance *when it was the only remaining choice.* In the absence of inspired leadership and without the spirit to die as a free people rather than be slaughtered as passive victims, most of the Jews never considered the option of survival in mountain refuges as a realistic choice.

If there is one universal lesson from the Slovak National Uprising it is this: Those who will engage in genocide have no conscience; they will not be dissuaded by diplomacy, appeals, or bribes. Until justice prevails in the world—and that is not likely to happen in this generation or the next—the potential victims have no other choice than to be prepared to resist and to do that competently. I am proud that I resisted the Nazis with force, and I am proud to have participated in the Slovak National Uprising. It convinced me that resistance to evil is the right thing to do. It is a cost we all must be always be willing to pay as the price of freedom.

A POSTSCRIPT

POSTSCRIPT

I left Trenčín for Paris in February 1948, and from there, I went on to London. I finally arrived in New York on October 15, 1948, a young emigrant with $26 in my pocket. I took a job selling socks at the Gertz department store in Jamaica, New York.

I graduated from the tuition-free Cooper Union in New York in 1953 with a degree in engineering. I then worked my way through M.I.T., receiving my master's in industrial management in 1955.

I have been married to Mona since 1954. Our union produced four children (Vera, Andrew, Steven, and the much admired and beloved Eric, who died in 1984). There are six grandchildren so far.

I started working with computers in 1954, which led to management positions in information technologies with progressively increasing responsibilities; I served as the chief information executive for General Foods, Kraft, Xerox, Department of Defense, and NASA.

At present, I hold the position of distinguished professor of information sciences at George Mason University's School of Information Technology and Engineering. I have also held an academic appointment as adjunct professor at the U.S. Military Academy at West Point.

I received the Defense Medal for Distinguished Public Service in 1993 (the Defense Department's highest civilian recognition). In 2002, I was honored as a recipient of the NASA Exceptional Service Medal.

Over the years, I have published five books and over 250 articles on information management and information worker productivity.

I will continue serving as a grateful citizen of my adopted country, the United States of America, as long as I can for giving me an opportunity to live in peace.

The text about the Trenčín years has existed in a scattered draft form for the past fifteen years. The time has come to assemble the text into a cohesive whole and see it published before the memories fade.

For the past sixty-five years, I have succeeded in diverting my thoughts from the past and concentrating entirely on building for the future. In my declining years, I decided to commit my remembrances of past events to writing. I offer herein a story that sometime, somewhere, someone may discover insights into how to cope with the hardships that will continue to be inflicted on generations to come as long as justice and freedom remain only a temporary blessing.